Testimonials

Fantastic insights, Christie! Your expertise shines through in demystifying blockchain interoperability. It's exciting to see how these innovations are shaping the future of finance and beyond. Keep up the great work!

> *-Joe F.*

Super clear breakdown, finally a blockchain explainer that doesn't make my brain hurt!

> *-MD F.*

Great overview! Love how you simplified complex concepts for broader understanding.

> *-Mahbub S.*

ALSO BY CHRISTIE RUSS

Amazon #1 Best Seller
The Power to Rise

Blockchain Made Simple

The Future of Everything

By Christie Russ

Published by:
Center for Creators
www.CenterForCreators.com

Identifiers
Library of Congress Control Number:
2025941381 (Hard Back) 2025941614 (Paperback)
ISBN:
979-8-9921378-5-9 (Hard Back) 979-8-9921378-8-0 (Paperback)

This book is intended for informational and inspirational purposes only. The author assumes no responsibility for any actions taken based on the content of this book.

Cover Design: Christie Russ

Editor: Center for Creators

First Edition: September 2025
Printed in the United States of America

Disclaimer

The information provided in this book is for educational and inspirational purposes only. It is not a substitute for professional advice, including but not limited to legal, financial, medical, or therapeutic guidance. The author and publisher assume no responsibility for any actions, decisions, or outcomes resulting from the use of this book's content. Readers are encouraged to consult licensed professionals for advice tailored to their specific circumstances.

"The future belongs to those who believe in the beauty of their dreams."

— **Eleanor Roosevelt**

Table of Contents

Part 1: Foundations of Blockchain and Digital Assets

Understanding the fundamentals that make blockchain so powerful.

1. What is Blockchain?

A beginner-friendly breakdown of what blockchain actually is, how it works, and why it's being called the foundation of the next digital revolution.

2. The Function of Tokens: Why Every Blockchain Needs One

Tokens aren't just digital currency, they're the mechanism that secures, governs, and sustains decentralized systems.

3. What Gives a Token Value in the Blockchain Economy

Tokens gain value through movement, utility, and liquidity. This chapter explores how decentralized exchanges, AMMs, and community participation shape the foundation of token economics.

Part 3: The Future of Decentralization and the Global Economy

Where blockchain is taking us next, and why it matters for everyone.

32. How to Prepare for a Decentralized World

A practical exploration of how to adapt, participate, and thrive as power shifts from centralized control to distributed networks.

33. The Beginning of Everything: A Final Note on Vision, Growth, and Empowerment

A closing reflection on why understanding this technology now means stepping boldly into the future with knowledge, purpose, and power.

Introduction

What if the next global revolution does not come from a government, a law, or an institution, but from the invisible upgrade already reshaping our digital lives?

You are already part of it, even if you have not noticed.

It is called blockchain, and it is not just about cryptocurrency. It is about power, trust, and ownership in a digital world that is changing faster than anyone expected.

When I first stepped into this space in 2018, I was not a programmer. I was not a tech investor. I was an intuitive strategist and personal transformation advisor, guiding people through personal evolution, not code.

But something massive was unfolding right in front of me.

A new digital foundation was being built, one that could support not just new technologies, but new systems of value, identity, and freedom. And I realized:

If we wait to understand it, we will be forced to adapt to it.
But if we learn now, we can lead.

That is why I created this book.

Because blockchain is no longer about hype or headlines. It is quietly becoming the infrastructure behind everything: how we buy homes, how we prove who we are, how we earn, how we vote, how we trust. And yet, most people still think it is too complex to understand, so they ignore it or assume it does not apply to them.

It does.

This book is not about investing. It is about understanding.

It is about making sense of the invisible transformation that is happening around you and showing you how to claim your place in it.

Inside, you will find:

- Real-world examples of how blockchain is being used today.
- Simple, clear breakdowns of the technology (no jargon).
- Stories that connect blockchain to everyday life: buying. groceries, proving your identity, tracking a shipment, or owning something digitally.
- Insights that show how it is affecting your future and how to prepare for it.

You will also meet the deeper mission behind my work, why I created the CFC Token in 2021, how it went viral within weeks, and why I believe blockchain is not just about data or decentralization, it is about human evolution.

The internet changed how we connect.
Blockchain will change how we own, how we trust, and how we grow.

This book is for the everyday person who is ready to understand the future and own their place in it.

Let us begin.

—

Christie Russ
Founder of Center for Creators
Amazon #1 Bestselling Author of *The Power to Rise*

Part 1

Foundations of Blockchain and Digital Assets

Understanding the fundamentals that make blockchain so powerful.

Chapter 1

What is Blockchain?

A beginner-friendly breakdown of what blockchain actually is, how it works, and why it's being called the foundation of the next digital revolution.

Before We Knew the Internet Would Change Everything

It is the early 1990s. Someone tells you that, in just a few years, you will be sending letters without a stamp, shopping without leaving your house, and holding face-to-face meetings with people halfway around the world from a small device in your pocket.

Most people laughed.

The internet sounded like science fiction. It was slow, hard to use, and had no obvious purpose for the average person. But a small group of people saw what it could become. They did not just see a new technology. They saw a new world. These people were not lucky. They were early. They were informed. And that made all the difference.

Today, blockchain is at that same tipping point.

You have probably heard the term. You might have seen it connected to cryptocurrency headlines. It may sound technical, confusing, or irrelevant to your life.

That is exactly what many thought about the internet.

But behind the noise, something much bigger is happening.

Blockchain is already reshaping the systems we use every day including finance, healthcare, identity, supply chains, education, and government. Soon, you will not be able to avoid it. Not because it will be in your face, but because it will be working quietly behind the scenes, much like the software updates that improve your phone while you sleep.

Think of blockchain as a global software update. One that upgrades how trust, value, and identity operate across every sector, not just your personal device. It runs quietly in the background, but its effects are transformative, rewriting the rules of ownership and access in the digital age.

So, What Is Blockchain?

At its core, blockchain is a new way to store and verify information.

Think of it as a digital notebook, except instead of one person writing in it and keeping it hidden away, it is shared across thousands of computers around the world. Every time something new is written, it is time-stamped, locked in, and verified by a network of computers working together to ensure the data is accurate and consistent. Once written, it cannot be erased, edited, or tampered with.

That is the core innovation: security through transparency.

Unlike a traditional database run by a bank, a company, or a government, a blockchain is decentralized. It does not belong to anyone, and that is exactly what makes it powerful.

How It Works (Without the Tech Headache)

Here is the simplest way to understand it:

- A block contains information. That could be a payment, a contract, a vote, or even proof of identity.

- Once that block is full, it is sealed and linked to the previous block, creating a chain.

- This chain of blocks is stored not in one place, but on thousands of computers globally.

- If someone tries to change a block, the system checks all the copies. If one does not match the rest, it is rejected.

This is what makes blockchain nearly impossible to hack or falsify. No central server. No single point of failure. No need to trust any one party.

You trust the mathematical rules and cryptographic algorithms that govern how the system operates. You trust the transparency. You trust the network.

Now that you have the big picture, let's break down the actual steps of how a blockchain transaction moves from start to finish.

How Blockchain Works: Step by Step

1. A transaction begins

Someone decides to send value, share data, or trigger an action (for example, sending cryptocurrency, proving identity, or updating supply chain records).

2. The transaction is broadcast

This information is sent to a network of computers, called *nodes*, that all maintain a copy of the blockchain.

3. The transaction is verified

Nodes check that the transaction is valid. For money transfers, this means confirming the sender has the funds. For data, it means confirming the rules are followed.

4. The transaction is grouped into a block

Valid transactions are bundled together in a "block." Each block contains:

- The list of new transactions

- A timestamp

- A reference (hash) to the previous block

5. Consensus is reached

The network agrees on which transactions are real using a *consensus mechanism*:

- **Proof of Work**: computers solve puzzles to validate the block

- **Proof of Stake**: validators "stake" tokens to secure the block

6. The block is added to the chain

Once consensus is reached, the new block is permanently added to the chain of prior blocks. This is why it is called a *blockchain*.

7. The record becomes immutable

Because each block links to the one before it, changing anything would require rewriting the entire chain — making blockchain tamper-resistant and trusted.

8. Tokens power the system

Tokens play a key role in keeping blockchains running:

- They pay transaction fees (gas)

- They reward validators or miners for securing the network

- They align incentives so participants act honestly

9. The transaction is complete

The recipient sees the result (value received, identity verified, record updated), and the blockchain ledger is updated everywhere at once.

Why Is Blockchain Such a Big Deal?

Today, most of our systems depend on middlemen to approve, verify, or record things:

- Banks process your payments

- Governments verify your identity

- Lawyers validate your contracts

- Platforms manage your content

- Real estate agents transfer property ownership

- Healthcare providers store and share your records

- Insurance companies verify claims and assess risk

These institutions slow things down, add costs, and still get breached, corrupted, or delayed.

Blockchain changes that.

It allows direct, tamper-proof, trustless transactions, not because you trust the other person, but because you trust the system.

It is already being used to:

- Track products from factory to shelf, stopping counterfeit goods and verifying ethical sourcing

- Protect medical records so patients, not corporations, control their data

- Enable digital voting with auditable, unchangeable records

- Verify authenticity of luxury goods, digital art, and even real estate titles

And now, major real-world projects are proving its potential:

- **Walmart and IBM** use blockchain to track food supply chains from farms to shelves, reducing the time it takes to trace contaminated produce from days to seconds

- **Estonia's e-Government** secures health records, identity data, and public services through blockchain, making it one of the most digitally advanced nations in the world

- **MIT** issues blockchain-based diplomas, allowing graduates to share verifiable credentials instantly with employers

- **UN World Food Programme** uses blockchain to deliver food and financial aid directly to refugees, ensuring transparency and reducing fraud

- **HSBC and Wells Fargo** have used blockchain to settle cross-border foreign exchange transactions in real time, eliminating the delays and costs of traditional clearing systems

If It Sounds Complicated, So Did the Internet

It is okay if this feels like a lot. Think back again to the early internet.

In the beginning, you had to:

- Use dial-up tones and command lines

- Memorize strange addresses

- Trust a process no one really understood

But as the technology improved, all of that faded into the background.

Today, you do not "use the internet" you just live on it. You send an email, tap an app, or order a meal. It works invisibly.

Blockchain will evolve the same way.

Right now, it still feels early. There are extra steps and extra friction. But that is a feature of today's version, not tomorrows.

Already, developers are building seamless blockchain tools that work just like the apps you already use. They are hiding the complexity and elevating the benefit.

The same way your phone updates itself without asking for your input, blockchain will quietly upgrade our systems behind the scenes until its benefits are so normal that we no longer notice the change.

The Bottom Line: It Is a New Foundation

Blockchain is not just about digital currencies.

It is about something much bigger.

It is about trust, access, identity, ownership, speed, and transparency without needing permission.

It is the digital foundation of the next internet.

The foundation for:

- Faster global payments without banks
  Payments can be made in seconds at any time of day with minimal fees without relying on banks or clearinghouses.

- Transparent supply chains without delays
  Every item can be tracked from origin to delivery, allowing consumers and businesses to verify authenticity, reduce fraud, and identify inefficiencies.

- Identity that belongs to you, not a platform
  With blockchain, you can carry your own digital ID, giving you control over your credentials without handing them over to corporations or governments.

- Ownership that cannot be faked
  Whether it is real estate, digital art, or intellectual property, blockchain provides tamper-proof proof of ownership that anyone can verify.

- Value that can be transferred without borders
  Blockchain makes it possible to send money, assets, or data to anyone anywhere in the world without middlemen, restrictions, or delays.

Why It Matters That You Understand This Now

You do not need to become a blockchain developer.
You do not need to invest in cryptocurrency.

But it is beneficial to understand the technology because it is already reshaping the world around you. Those who understand it early are positioned to lead, adapt, and thrive as change accelerates.

This is more than a technology shift.
It is a shift in power.

Key Takeaways

- Blockchain is a decentralized, transparent, and secure way to store and verify information without relying on a single authority

- It builds trust through mathematics and distributed consensus rather than institutions

- Real-world use cases include finance, healthcare, education, supply chains, government services, and humanitarian aid

- Leading global organizations like Walmart, IBM, MIT, HSBC, and the UN are already using blockchain in high-impact ways

- Understanding blockchain now positions individuals and institutions to adapt and lead as it becomes embedded in everyday systems

---

Reflection Questions

1. How do the early days of the internet help explain where blockchain technology is today

2. Which of the global examples of blockchain use feel most relevant to your field of interest or study

3. What impact could blockchain have on reducing inefficiencies in industries you interact with regularly

4. How might a decentralized identity system change the way you share and protect your personal information

5. What opportunities could arise for you personally or professionally by understanding blockchain before it becomes fully mainstream

WHAT IS BLOCKCHAIN?

Transactions are grouped into blocks

Blocks are linked together in order

Data is secured with cryptography

Copies exist on thousands of computers

No single point of failure

Tamper-resistant & trustless

Chapter 2

The Function of Tokens: Why Every Blockchain Needs One

Tokens are more than currency, they are the mechanisms that allow blockchains to function, stay secure, and evolve without central authority.

A City Without a Mayor

Imagine a city with no mayor, no board of directors, and no central agency, yet somehow the lights stay on, the roads get maintained, and every resident plays a role in its success. There are no top-down orders, but things run smoothly because everyone is rewarded for showing up and participating.

That isn't just a metaphor. That's how a well-designed blockchain operates.

At the center of this self-organizing system is the token. It's not just a coin or investment vehicle, it's the core mechanism that allows a decentralized network to coordinate, verify transactions, prevent fraud, and evolve.

Without tokens, a blockchain is just code sitting in the dark. With them, it becomes a living, evolving economy of trust.

What Tokens Actually Do

Decentralized systems still need governance, rules, and incentives. Without central authority, the only way to keep things working fairly is to create a system of earned participation and automatic accountability.

Tokens make this possible by enabling five essential functions:

1. Deciding Who Validates Transactions

In centralized systems, you trust a bank, a credit card processor, or PayPal to process transactions. In a decentralized system, there's no middleman, so who decides what's valid?

That's where validators (or miners) come in. But to participate, they need skin in the game.

In Proof-of-Stake networks like Ethereum, Solana, or Cardano, validators must "stake" tokens as collateral. This stake increases their chance of being chosen to validate transactions. If they act dishonestly, they lose part or all of their tokens.

In Proof-of-Work systems like Bitcoin, miners use expensive computing power and electricity to solve puzzles and validate transactions. Cheating is financially self-defeating.

In both models, tokens create a self-enforcing economic system where trust is replaced by incentives.

2. Punishing Bad Actors

Blockchains can't call the police. They don't need to. They use tokens to create real consequences for dishonesty.

If a validator tries to game the system, they're automatically penalized, either by slashing their stake or by losing the energy and resources they spent trying to cheat.

The fear of loss keeps people honest. That's how blockchains protect themselves.

3. **Managing Upgrades and Evolution**

Blockchains need to evolve, but who decides what gets updated when there's no CEO?

Token holders do. Many blockchains allow token holders to vote on proposed changes, upgrades, or parameters. The more tokens you hold, the more influence you have.

This makes governance transparent and community-driven, without requiring a central authority.

4. **Powering the Ecosystem**

Tokens are also used to power everything built on top of a blockchain like apps, games, marketplaces, and smart contracts.

Think of tokens like fuel. If someone wants to run a decentralized application, execute a smart contract, or send data, they pay a small fee in tokens. These fees reward validators and keep the network running efficiently.

This creates a self-sustaining system that rewards builders and users alike.

5. **Creating Incentives for Growth**

Without marketing departments or paid user acquisition, how do decentralized networks grow?

By rewarding early users and contributors with tokens.

This is what allowed platforms like Uniswap or Aave to explode in popularity. They gave real ownership to the people helping build them, developers, users, and even content creators.

Tokens don't just fuel activity, they reward participation, turning users into stakeholders.

Real-World Use Cases: Tokens in Action

To fully understand the impact of tokens, it helps to look at how they're being used right now.

Helium: Decentralized Wireless and 5G

Helium allows individuals to set up wireless hotspots and build 5G infrastructure. In return, they earn HNT and MOBILE tokens. This crowdsourced network bypasses telecom giants and puts the power of connectivity in the hands of everyday people.

The Graph: Making Blockchain Data Searchable

Blockchains store vast amounts of raw data. The Graph indexes that data so developers can query it efficiently. Those who run indexing nodes earn GRT tokens—making the entire data infrastructure of Web3 possible.

Arweave: Permanent, Uncensorable Storage

Arweave stores files permanently. Users pay once in AR tokens, and their data lives forever—unchanged, uncensored, and accessible. It's like a blockchain version of the Library of Congress.

Chainlink: Bringing Off-Chain Data On-Chain

Chainlink provides trusted data to smart contracts, like stock prices, weather reports, or election results. Operators stake LINK tokens to guarantee reliability. If they lie, they lose their stake.

XRP and the XRP Ledger: Fast, Borderless Value Transfer

The XRP Ledger requires a tiny XRP fee for each transaction. This prevents spam and keeps the network efficient. XRP also acts as a bridge currency, allowing instant conversion between fiat currencies. It's not theoretical, it's running in live enterprise environments worldwide.

Beyond Price

Tokens are often seen as speculative assets—but that's missing the point.

They're not here to make headlines. They're here to make decentralized systems work.

Tokens are the incentives, the punishment, the governance, the fuel, and the ownership structure all wrapped into one.

They replace top-down control with community coordination. They allow innovation to scale without corporate gatekeeping.

They make the internet functional again—this time without giving all the power to a handful of companies.

The Bigger Picture

Tokens aren't an add-on or a bonus. They are not an extra feature. They are what makes blockchain work.

Without tokens, blockchain would just be a ledger. With tokens, it becomes a self-governing, self-securing, self-sustaining economy.

Without tokens:

- There is no way to secure the network
- No method for reaching consensus

- No spam protection

- No way to upgrade

- No reason for anyone to participate

With tokens:

- A decentralized economy comes to life

- Everyone has a stake

- The system grows through contribution, not control

Tokens are not part of the system. They are the system. We are watching value itself become programmable and participatory.

We're not just watching industries evolve; we're seeing value itself get redefined.

Key Takeaways

- Tokens are essential to how blockchains function. They provide security, coordination, governance, participation, and protection.

- Without tokens, a blockchain cannot maintain trust, reward contributors, or prevent abuse.

- Real-world projects like Helium, The Graph, Chainlink, and Arweave demonstrate how tokens extend blockchain's power into physical infrastructure.

- XRP is a core example of a native token that enables fast, low-cost, cross-border payments and protects the network against spam.

Reflection Questions

1. What systems in your world depend on middlemen, and how could tokens remove those layers?

2. How might token-based participation shift how people contribute to technology, platforms, or communities?

3. Which token-powered use case feels most relevant to your life or business right now, and why?

Chapter 3

What Gives a Token Value in the Blockchain Economy

Tokens gain value through movement, utility, and liquidity. This chapter explores how decentralized exchanges, AMMs, and community participation shape the foundation of token economics.

In the traditional financial world, value is controlled from the top. Currencies gain legitimacy because governments issued them. Companies become valuable because they posted profits and filed reports. Access to these systems is limited. Central banks, investment firms, and regulatory agencies act as gatekeepers, controlling how money moves, who can participate, and what is considered trustworthy.

Blockchain flips that model. In this new decentralized economy, value is not assigned by institutions. It is created by participation. A token gains value when people use it, trade it, build with it, and believe in its function. Movement is no longer a byproduct of value; it is the source of it.

This chapter explores how tokens in the blockchain economy gain value through activity, liquidity, and utility. We'll look at the roles of automated market makers (AMMs), liquidity pools, and stablecoin pairings. We'll examine how meme coins gain momentum through culture, how decentralized exchanges create flow, and why participation is now the most powerful form of trust.

The Shift from Centralized to Decentralized Value

In centralized systems, value flows through authority. A bank note is worth something because a government says so. A stock has value because it represents ownership in a company with provable financials. If a centralized party doesn't validate the asset, it's considered speculative at best or worthless at worst.

Blockchain economies are built differently. A token does not need to be backed by a central bank or represent a claim on future profits. Its value emerges from how it operates inside a decentralized ecosystem. This includes:

- How easily it can be traded

- How much liquidity is available

- How many people are using it in real-world applications

- How actively it's being built into products, platforms, or protocols

In a decentralized system, a token is only as strong as its ability to move. Movement is trust. Movement is proof.

From Fiat to Function

Fiat currencies maintain value because they are legal tender, enforced by law. Stocks are valued based on performance and projected earnings. But blockchain tokens are often not tied to a single jurisdiction or company. Their value is based on use.

If a token powers a rewards platform, and people want access to those rewards, it gains value. BAT (Basic Attention Token), for example, is used to reward users and content creators within the Brave browser ecosystem.

If it allows access to a private community, and that access is in demand, it gains value. GRT (The Graph) is used to access and query blockchain data across networks like Ethereum, powering decentralized apps and developer tools.

If it's required to pay network fees or deploy smart contracts, it gains value. XRP is used to pay transaction fees, provide liquidity for cross-border payments, and serve as a bridge currency on the XRP Ledger's decentralized exchange. VET, the native token of VeChain, is used to generate VTHO, which powers transactions and smart contract execution on its enterprise supply chain network.

If it moves between wallets, exchanges, and applications with high volume and speed, it gains value.

Tokens in this ecosystem represent more than digital money. They represent energy in motion, a signal of trust, action, and potential.

AMMs and Liquidity Pools: The Infrastructure of Movement

One of the most powerful innovations in blockchain finance is the **automated market maker** (AMM). In traditional finance, exchanges rely on order books. A buyer offers to purchase an asset at a certain price. A seller agrees to sell at that price. If no match exists, the trade doesn't happen. Often, professional market makers step in to fill this gap, ensuring liquidity and reducing price gaps.

Blockchain removes the middlemen. With AMMs, trades don't require a matching buyer and seller. Instead, smart contracts allow users to instantly swap between two tokens, using funds provided by the community.

This happens through **liquidity pools**, reserves of two tokens locked into a smart contract. For example:

• A XRP/RLUSD pool lets users swap between XRP and a dollar-pegged stablecoin
• A UNI/ETH pool allows trading between Uniswap's governance token and Ethereum
• A LINK/MATIC pool enables movement between Chainlink and Polygon's native asset

Emerging projects like the CFC Token or The Pickleball Coin (PBC) also use AMM strategies to create access, fuel participation, and support digital community ecosystems.

Users who deposit equal values of each token into the pool are called liquidity providers. In return, they receive a share of the trading fees. More importantly, they enable the token to move freely.

The pool itself becomes the counterparty to every trade.

Why Movement Equals Value

A token that does not move has no utility. It becomes stagnant. Movement gives a token visibility. It shows that people are interacting with it, trusting it, and circulating it through the ecosystem.

Tokens that move consistently often gain:

- **More stable pricing** through increased supply and demand balancing

- **More integration** with wallets, platforms, and apps

- **More investor confidence** as data shows consistent activity

- **More utility** as projects recognize the value of building with active assets

Movement creates momentum, and momentum builds belief.

Liquidity as a Signal of Confidence

Liquidity pools are not just tools for trading, they are real-time signals of belief.

When users lock their assets into a liquidity pool, they're demonstrating that they trust the token will remain useful and relevant. The deeper the liquidity, the more stable the price and the smoother the trading experience.

High liquidity shows:

- Community support

- Long-term engagement

- Trust in the token's purpose and future use

Projects with shallow liquidity pools often suffer from high price volatility, poor user experience, and low adoption. Projects with strong, active pools become magnetic, drawing in new users, developers, and collaborators.

The Power of Stablecoin Pairings

While any two tokens can be paired in a liquidity pool, some of the most effective pairings involve **stablecoins** like USDC, RLUSD, or EURC. These tokens maintain a consistent value, usually pegged to a fiat currency like the U.S. dollar.

When a utility token is paired with a stablecoin, it creates:

- **Reduced volatility** for traders

- **Faster entry points** for users who are used to fiat pricing

- **Greater appeal** for institutions and first-time buyers

Stablecoin pairings anchor a token to something familiar. This increases confidence and opens the door to broader adoption.

Projects like Stellar, Circle, and Ripple have actively promoted stablecoin strategies for this reason. They recognize that reducing friction is key to increasing flow, and that flow is what gives a token life.

The Meme Coin Phenomenon

Not every token gains value through traditional use cases. Some gain it through culture.

Meme coins like PEPE and Floki started as jokes but became billion-dollar assets. Their value doesn't come from smart contracts or utility. It comes from community energy and viral attention.

Meme coins gain traction because they tap into:

- Internet humor

- Collective identity

- Speculative excitement

- Influencer amplification

While often volatile, these tokens follow the same rules of movement. As they are traded across platforms, listed on exchanges, and discussed in media, they generate liquidity. That liquidity becomes value.

Even without formal use cases, meme coins prove that in blockchain, belief and movement can be enough to create momentum.

From DEX Offers to 24/7 Trading

Before AMMs became widespread, decentralized trading depended on DEX offers. These were manual listings where users set a buy or sell price and waited for someone to match them. It was peer-to-peer trading in its rawest form, functional, but inefficient.

AMMs changed everything. They introduced continuous, instant trading. They removed the need for timing, coordination, or perfect pricing. Now, users could swap tokens at any time with no gatekeepers involved.

This shift was more than technical, it was philosophical. It made access continuous. It made value fluid. And it allowed new tokens to grow without needing approval from centralized platforms or major investors.

AMMs democratized liquidity. And in doing so, they helped unlock a new standard of token growth.

The Real Foundation of Token Value

Across every example, from stablecoins and meme coins to community tokens and platform utilities, the theme is the same.

Value comes from function, trust, and flow.

- If people use a token, it gains relevance.

- If it moves smoothly through exchanges, it gains confidence.

- If it anchors a rewards system, governance structure, or global platform, it gains long-term strength.

Blockchain didn't just decentralize money. It decentralized the process of value creation itself. Tokens are no longer waiting for permission. Their value comes from what they enable, and how many people are willing to participate in that vision.

Key Takeaways

• Token value in blockchain ecosystems is built through use, liquidity, and movement, not through centralized authority or financial reports.

• Automated market makers (AMMs) and liquidity pools create the infrastructure for token trading without requiring a buyer and seller to match.

• Liquidity pools signal confidence in a token's future and determine how easily it can be exchanged.

• Stablecoin pairings reduce volatility and make tokens more accessible to new users and institutions.

• Meme coins demonstrate how culture and community energy can generate real value through attention and trade volume.

• Value in the blockchain economy is participatory, it grows through trust, activity, and usefulness.

Reflection Questions

1. Which aspects of token value, utility, liquidity, or belief resonate most with how you assign value in your daily life?

2. Have you ever supported or joined a project before it became widely accepted? What drove your decision to participate early?

3. How do you see your role evolving in a world where value is created from the bottom up instead of issued from the top down?

4. What might change in your business, community, or industry if participation replaced permission as the measure of worth?

Chapter 4

The Application of Digital Assets: How They Bring Blockchain to Life

Digital assets fuel automation, enable trustless systems, and expand blockchain's power into industries like finance, healthcare, and global trade.

From theory to isle three

Blockchain shifted from theory to reality for me one afternoon in a Sam's Club warehouse store. Just days earlier I had read about VeChain's partnership with Walmart China, where blockchain tokens document each checkpoint in the supply chain, from farm to processing facility to retail shelf. The article focused on transparency and trust, not price speculation.

Walking past rows of chilled cases, I noticed a statement painted across the back wall of the meat department:

"Responsibly Sourced for Premium Quality."

The words echoed what I had just learned: quality rooted in traceable data. In that moment I saw how digital assets turn supply chains into visible, verifiable stories. Blockchain wasn't waiting for tomorrow, it was already upgrading systems I use every day.

Digital Assets: The Invisible Engine

Digital assets are not simply a new form of currency. They are the active force that brings blockchain technology into motion, transforming it from a static database into a living, functional ecosystem that powers industries across the globe. These assets allow blockchain networks to move, adapt, and evolve without requiring traditional intermediaries or institutions.

While the headlines often focus on Bitcoin or Ethereum as investment opportunities, the true value of digital assets lies in what they enable. Without them, blockchains could not operate securely, fairly, or efficiently. These assets ensure that users can verify transactions, execute smart contracts, exchange value, and interact with decentralized applications, all within a trustless, automated framework.

Digital Assets: Beyond Currency

At the core, a digital asset is a programmable unit of value created on a blockchain. But that value isn't limited to money. It can represent ownership, access, identity, or participation. These assets are the connective tissue between the code and the world it serves.

For example:

- On Ethereum, digital assets are used to power decentralized finance (DeFi), enabling lending, borrowing, and trading without banks.

- On VeChain, tokens validate supply chains and track authenticity across logistics, pharmaceuticals, and luxury goods.

- On the XRP Ledger, XRP enables global value transfers and secures the network from spam.

Digital assets are not just tools for speculation. They are functional components in networks that demand security, coordination, automation, and transparency.

Real-World Applications

Digital assets are already transforming how we interact with the world. These use cases demonstrate how blockchain moves beyond theory into real utility:

1. **Supply Chain and Product Integrity**

   Platforms like VeChain and IBM Food Trust use tokens to track goods from origin to destination. In industries such as food safety, pharmaceuticals, and fashion, digital assets verify where a product has been, what it contains, and whether it meets regulatory standards. This transparency prevents fraud and protects consumers.

2. **Identity and Data Ownership**

   Digital identity platforms use blockchain-based assets to give individuals control over their credentials, logins, and health records. Instead of storing identity with centralized authorities, users can present verifiable proofs through tokens. This is already being piloted in education, healthcare, and public infrastructure.

3. **Global Payments and Currency Conversion**

   Cross-border payments are slow and expensive in traditional systems. Digital assets like XRP simplify this by serving as bridge currencies, allowing institutions to move value instantly without pre-funded accounts or costly intermediaries.

4. **Healthcare Data and Access**

   Digital assets are beginning to power secure, permissioned access to patient data. Blockchain platforms are enabling systems where patients control who sees their health records, and medical providers can verify accuracy and consent in real time.

5. **Smart Contracts and Decentralized Applications**

   Smart contracts need digital assets to execute. From real estate to insurance to legal agreements, tokens serve as the mechanism that allows contracts to self-trigger based on conditions met, eliminating manual processing, reducing delays, and removing middlemen.

The Flow of Tokens and Services in the Blockchain Economy

Imagine Walmart is buying a shipment of lettuce from a farm. Traditionally, this process involves paperwork, phone calls, and waiting days for banks and shipping companies to update their records. With blockchain, the entire process can be simplified and secured.

1. **Token Creation (Digital Twin):**

    On the blockchain, a digital token is created to represent the shipment of lettuce. This is not a cryptocurrency but an *asset token*, a digital twin of the real product. It contains details like the farm it came from, harvest date, and certification of safety.

2. **Tracking the Shipment:**

    As the lettuce moves through the supply chain, from the farm, to the truck, to the distribution center, the digital twin token is updated with each step. This creates a transparent and tamper-proof history of where the lettuce has been and under what conditions it was stored.

3. **Payment with Currency Tokens:**

    When Walmart receives the lettuce and confirms that it meets all quality and safety standards, a smart contract automatically releases payment through a currency token such as a stablecoin. Instead of waiting days for a bank transfer to clear, the farmer or supplier is paid immediately once delivery conditions are met. This not only speeds up the process but also ensures fairness, since payment is directly tied to proof of delivery and verified data on the blockchain.

4. **Verification and Services:**

   Regulators, logistics providers, and even consumers can verify the entire journey of the lettuce through the blockchain, ensuring transparency and trust at every step. Smart contracts can also trigger additional services automatically, such as releasing insurance coverage if the shipment is delayed, updating Walmart's inventory records when goods arrive, or alerting regulators if safety requirements are not met. This automation removes delays, reduces human error, and builds confidence across every participant in the supply chain.

How Digital Assets Unlock Usefulness

Without digital assets, blockchain would remain a passive tool, a database with no way to act, incentivize, or evolve. These assets bring the system to life, transforming it into something interactive, engaging, and adaptable to the real world.

Here's how:

- **Enable Permissioned Access:** Digital assets grant access to private content, restricted files, or VIP areas in applications, events, or games. They act like programmable keys.

- **Automate Verification:** A token can represent a license, degree, or certificate. Instead of relying on a middleman to validate a credential, a digital asset proves it instantly.

- **Drive User Participation:** Platforms reward content creation, user feedback, or voting with tokens—creating feedback loops that keep users engaged and valued.

- **Trigger Utility:** In dApps, assets can unlock levels, activate features, or execute rights. Whether it's upgrading software, opening gated content, or distributing royalties.

- **Track Contributions:** Artists, developers, or researchers can use tokens to receive fair distribution of earnings or attributions in collaborative environments.

These are not passive holdings. Digital assets move, respond, and evolve with the user.

Key Takeaway

- Digital assets serve as the fuel that powers blockchain systems, enabling them to operate with trust and automation.
- They are not speculative by design, they are essential infrastructure for real-world applications.
- Without digital assets, blockchain would remain static code. With them, it becomes a dynamic, decentralized system of value.

Reflection Questions

1. Where in your life or industry could digital assets simplify processes or improve transparency?

2. How might your perception of cryptocurrency change if you focus on function rather than price?

3. What areas of society could benefit most from decentralized ownership and automated trust?

4. Which real-world application of digital assets resonates most with you, and why?

5. How might digital assets reshape how you access, verify, or protect valuable information?

Chapter 5

Beyond Money: How Digital Assets Are Transforming Industries

Digital assets are powering automation, enhancing security, and enabling new forms of ownership across global industries. This chapter explores how they are reshaping systems from the inside out.

Infrastructure in Motion

Imagine living in a world where the systems around you are no longer run on outdated paperwork, siloed databases, or sluggish approvals. Instead, they pulse with invisible intelligence where decisions are automated, records self-verify, and value moves the moment it's created. That's not a prediction. It's already happening. And it's being powered by digital assets you'll likely never see.

By now, you understand that blockchain isn't just about cryptocurrency. You've seen how tokens secure networks and how digital assets bring blockchain systems to life. But there's a deeper transformation underway, one where these assets are embedding themselves into the operational fabric of entire industries. In this chapter, we move from *what* digital assets are to *how* they're silently upgrading the world around you.

This is about infrastructure.

The Silent Infrastructure Behind Everyday Systems

Most infrastructure doesn't demand attention, it enables flow. Roads, plumbing, and electrical grids fade into the background until they stop working. In the same way, digital assets are becoming the silent infrastructure behind how industries operate, transact, and evolve.

This isn't limited to crypto wallets or investment platforms. Digital assets are being integrated into global trade, insurance automation, identity verification, credentialing, supply chain traceability, and environmental impact tracking.

You may never see these systems directly. But soon, you'll feel them in faster approvals, cleaner data, real-time updates, and systems that just work without friction. That's the mark of infrastructure that's doing its job.

The Real Upgrade Is Automation at the Edge

One of the least understood powers of digital assets is their ability to activate processes without needing a central trigger. With smart contracts and decentralized logic, decisions can be made at the edge of the network.

Think of a shipping container arriving at a port. Instead of someone manually checking a clipboard, a sensor detects its arrival, verifies the seal is unbroken, confirms the humidity level stayed within range, and automatically releases payment from the buyer to the seller. All of that can happen without a single human needing to lift a pen. The logic is pre-coded, the data is live, and the asset that triggers the transaction already exists on-chain.

Now apply this to global finance. Environmental compliance. Real estate title transfers. Disaster relief. Even voting. Digital assets don't just move value, they activate systems.

Tokenizing Processes, Not Just Products

The conversation around tokenization has often centered on turning real-world things into digital representations like property, art, or collectibles. But the true power lies in tokenizing processes.

When a digital asset represents a step in a process, it can be tracked, verified, and actioned on without needing centralized oversight. This has profound implications:

- In healthcare, digital assets tied to medical credentials can verify a provider's authority without a licensing board needing to intervene.

- In sustainability, sensor data combined with tokenized rewards can encourage responsible behavior from recycling to emissions reductions.

- In education, achievements can be stored as verifiable credentials, accessible globally and free from institutional gatekeeping.

The result? Systems that are not only more efficient, but more open, responsive, and trusted.

A System That Pays Attention

In the traditional economy, most of your contributions go unnoticed. You don't get rewarded for how many hours you research before a purchase. You're not compensated for giving feedback to your doctor's office. You certainly don't earn anything for choosing a more sustainable shipping method.

Digital assets change that.

They allow systems to track, reward, and adapt to human behavior in real time. They make it possible for people to become participants, not just users. And they create loops of value that incentivize quality, care, and conscious action.

Imagine a fitness program that pays you when you move. A transportation system that rewards passengers for off-peak travel. A content platform that shares revenue based on the value your attention brings. These aren't ideas. They're already launching.

The Shift from Ownership to Interaction

Traditionally, infrastructure is about ownership, who owns the land, the pipeline, the broadband. But in the digital asset economy, infrastructure is about interaction.

The most valuable systems will be those that adapt, reward, and evolve based on engagement. In this world:

- Protocols that reward contributors can evolve faster.

- Networks that share value with users can grow stronger.

- Platforms that tokenize actions, not just assets, can reach further.

This is infrastructure that moves with us, not just under us.

The Foundation for What Comes Next

As we prepare to move into the next chapters, where blockchain is not just enhancing industries but redefining identity, ownership, and economics, it's important to recognize that digital assets are not a side note in this transformation. They are the fuel. The language. The coordination layer.

You won't always see them. But when a system works better than expected, when fraud is blocked, when delivery is instant, when your credentials sync across borders, you'll know they're there.

What This Means for You

This isn't just about technology. It is about how your life is already changing in ways you may not see yet. Blockchain is becoming the hidden system behind how you earn, spend, prove, and protect what matters most.

Your Money

Think about the frustration of waiting days for a paycheck to clear or losing part of your transfer to fees. With blockchain, money moves instantly and fully, straight into your hands, not lost in middle layers. It means more control, more security, and more of your hard-earned income staying with you.

Your Identity

Every time you log in, buy online, or fill out a form, you give away pieces of yourself to companies you barely know. Blockchain flips that power. You decide what to share, with whom, and for how long. Your identity becomes yours again, private, portable, and protected.

Your Health

Health records locked in old systems put your care at risk. Blockchain lets your medical history travel with you, securely and accurately. No more repeating details at every visit, no more missing files. Doctors see the whole picture so you can get better, faster care.

Your Choices

When you shop, how do you know what you are really bringing into your home? Blockchain makes the invisible visible, tracing food, clothing, and even jewelry back to their source. You know it is safe, ethical, and authentic before it ever reaches your hands.

Your Work and Learning

Every certificate, license, or training you complete is part of your life's value. Blockchain locks that value in place so it can never be questioned, lost, or faked. Employers and clients see proof instantly. Your work is recognized, and your payments flow directly without waiting or doubt.

Your Community and Future

The way we vote, fund projects, and build communities is shifting. Blockchain gives people a transparent way to pool resources, make decisions, and hold institutions accountable. It means a future where your voice carries real weight, and where power is shared rather than controlled.

The transformation of industries through digital assets is not just about efficiency or cost savings. It is about rewriting the rules of trust, access, and ownership in ways that affect how you work, shop, learn, and live. Whether it is food on your table, records at your doctor's office, or credentials that prove your expertise, blockchain is steadily weaving itself into the fabric of daily life. By seeing beyond speculation and recognizing how industries are already changing, you gain the foresight to adapt, engage, and thrive in this new era.

Key Takeaways:

- Digital assets are becoming invisible infrastructure, powering the backend of modern systems.

- They enable automation, verification, and trust without centralized intervention.

- Tokenizing processes, not just things, it creates more fluid, intelligent systems.

- Infrastructure is shifting from ownership to interaction, rewarding those who contribute.

Reflection Questions:

1. What systems in your industry could be automated through tokenized processes?

2. How would your life change if your actions—wellness, feedback, attention—were recognized as valuable?

3. What legacy systems in your organization still rely on friction-heavy approvals or outdated tracking?

4. How could you begin to build with infrastructure that pays attention and adapts in real time?

Chapter 6

The Evolution of the Internet: Web 1, Web 2, and Web 3

Learn how the internet evolved from static pages to interactive platforms and how blockchain is ushering in a more decentralized and empowered Web3 era.

The Internet You Remember, and the One You're About to Meet

Think back to the first time you used the internet. Maybe it was dialing up on a bulky desktop, waiting for pages to load at a painfully slow speed. Or maybe you remember the first time you could interact with others online, post updates, or even shop from your phone. The internet has evolved drastically over the past few decades. We're now on the brink of another transformation, one that will change how we interact with the digital world forever.

The internet has gone through three major phases, known as Web 1, Web 2, and Web 3. Each phase has changed not only how we use technology but also who controls it. Understanding this shift helps put blockchain into perspective and shows why Web 3 is being called the future of the internet.

Web 1.0: The Read-Only Internet

The early days of the internet, from the late 1980s to the early 2000s, were what we now call Web 1.0. This was the read-only era, where the internet was basically a giant digital library.

Websites were static, meaning they didn't change or allow user interaction. The content was created and maintained by businesses, institutions, and early developers who had the resources and expertise to manage a digital presence.

There were no social media platforms, no user-generated content, simply basic pages with text and images. People visited sites to retrieve information, much like reading a newspaper or encyclopedia. The user's role was passive, limited to reading and viewing.

Companies and organizations controlled most of the content, and users could only consume information but not contribute to it. There was no comment section, no way to "like" something, and certainly no way to publish your own content without technical knowledge.

Web 1.0 was useful for looking up information, but it lacked the engagement and interactivity we expect today. It was efficient but sterile. Perfect for data retrieval, not for connection or creativity.

Web 2.0: The Social, Interactive Internet

In the early 2000s, the internet transformed into Web 2.0, the version we still use today. This was the birth of social media, user-generated content, and the ability to interact with websites rather than just reading them.

Platforms like Facebook, YouTube, Twitter, and later Instagram and TikTok changed everything by allowing people to create and share content. The internet became participatory. You didn't have to be a developer to have a voice.

E-commerce exploded, making it easier than ever to shop and conduct business online. Companies could target consumers with personalized ads, and people could launch businesses directly from their laptops.

Apps and cloud-based services allowed real-time collaboration, streaming, and instant communication. Users could edit documents together, hold video meetings, and store data in the cloud.

Web 2.0 gave people more freedom to engage, but it also centralized power in the hands of a few large companies. Tech giants like Google, Amazon, and Meta (formerly Facebook) built platforms where billions of people interact daily, but those same companies now control our data, privacy, and even what content we see.

We gained convenience, but lost control. Our data became the product, sold to advertisers, and used to train algorithms we don't fully understand. That's the trade-off that led to the next evolution.

Web 3.0: The Decentralized Internet

We are now entering the era of Web 3.0. It is transforming how financial transactions, contracts, identity, and ownership are managed online. Built on blockchain technology, Web 3 is designed to solve the core issues of Web 2.0, shifting control away from centralized tech giants and giving it back to users.

Decentralization means no single company or government controls the network. Instead of being stored in one place, data and systems are distributed across networks, reducing single points of failure and increasing transparency.

Users own their data. Instead of being stored on a company's servers, your data is encrypted and under your control. You decide what you share, with whom, and for how long. This is true digital ownership.

Smart contracts allow transactions and agreements to execute automatically, no middlemen, no delay. These contracts are built into the blockchain, and they perform actions only when pre-set conditions are met, ensuring security and speed.

People can earn directly from their content and contributions, instead of relying on advertisers or third-party platforms. Content creators, developers, and users are rewarded with digital assets that hold real value and can be traded, saved, or spent.

In Web 3, instead of logging into a site through a company like Google, users access platforms through blockchain-based identities that belong entirely to them. This identity follows them across applications, eliminating the need for dozens of usernames and passwords.

Why This Shift Matters

Web 3 isn't just a technology upgrade, it's a complete transformation in how we interact with the digital world. While Web 2 made it easy to create and share, it also required us to hand over control. Web 3 gives that control back.

Blockchain enables secure, peer-to-peer interactions without centralized oversight. This means more privacy, security, and financial autonomy.

The biggest innovation in Web 3 is its potential to reshape economies:

Decentralized finance (DeFi) allows users to lend, borrow, and earn without banks. These platforms are open to anyone, anywhere, and operate with full transparency on the blockchain.

Tokenized assets turn real-world value, like real estate or art, into digital tokens that can be bought, sold, or traded globally. This makes it possible for someone in Ghana to own a fraction of a property in Los Angeles.

Smart contracts remove the need for middlemen, slashing costs, and complexity. In industries like law, logistics, entertainment, and insurance, these self-executing agreements are speeding up deals and reducing fraud.

What's Holding Web 3 Back

Like any major shift, Web 3 adoption comes with challenges:

- **Usability** – Most blockchain platforms are still too complex for the average person. Wallets, private keys, gas fees—these terms and tools can be confusing, creating a barrier to entry.
- **Scalability** – Blockchain networks need to handle higher volumes to compete with traditional systems. Ethereum, for example, has faced congestion and high fees during peak usage.
- **Regulation** – Governments are still catching up and figuring out how to apply laws to these new systems. Some fear that unclear regulations may slow innovation or force companies to relocate.
- **Interoperability** – Different blockchain platforms must connect seamlessly to deliver a cohesive user experience. This is essential for users to move assets and data across networks effortlessly.

Despite these hurdles, Web 3 is gaining ground. Financial institutions, major tech companies, and even national governments are building blockchain solutions and preparing for this new internet era. Developers are working to build simpler interfaces, reduce fees, and improve accessibility for mainstream audiences.

Web3 Is Already Here

This transformation won't happen everywhere overnight. But make no mistake, Web3 is already here, quietly reshaping how we work, communicate, create, and thrive online. Those who understand it early won't just adapt to the future, they'll help define it. Web3 is already here and actively being integrated across industries.

While the full vision of a decentralized internet is still unfolding, many core elements of Web3 are already in use:

Decentralized finance (DeFi) is operating on platforms like Ethereum, Avalanche, and Solana.

Tokenized assets are being bought, sold, and traded globally, from real estate and stocks to art and music.

Smart contracts are powering insurance, lending, and logistics systems.

User-owned identities and wallets (like MetaMask, Phantom, and Ledger) are giving individuals control over their data and assets.

Major institutions like JPMorgan, Goldman Sachs, and Nike are already using Web3 tools (e.g., NFTs, blockchain payments, DeFi platforms).

Governments like Singapore and the UAE are rolling out blockchain-based digital identity programs and infrastructure upgrades.

So, while we are still in the early adoption curve, Web3 isn't a future fantasy, it's a living, evolving shift already reshaping finance, identity, ownership, and digital interaction.

The Future Is User-Owned

The move from Web 1 to Web 2 gave us interactivity, but at the cost of control. Web 3 aims to restore balance. It's not about replacing the internet. It's about rebuilding it with better architecture, where users own their data, control their identity, and benefit directly from their participation.

WEB 1.0

- STATIC PAGES
- READ-ONLY

WEB 2.0

- DYNAMIC CONTENT
- READ-WRITE

WEB 3.0

- DECENTRALIZED
- READ-WRITE-OWN

Key Takeaways

- Web 1.0 was static and informational, with limited user interaction.
- Web 2.0 introduced interactivity, social media, and user-generated content, but centralized power.
- Web 3.0 decentralizes control, returns ownership to users, and introduces blockchain-based identity, smart contracts, and new digital economies.
- The shift to Web 3 empowers individuals with privacy, ownership, and financial autonomy.

Reflection Questions

1. How do you see your digital life changing as Web 3 technologies become more common?

2. What would it mean to truly own your data and online identity?

3. How could decentralization change the way your industry operates?

4. What opportunities could Web 3 create for creators, consumers, or innovators like you?

Chapter 7

The Power of Blockchain Interoperability

What happens when different blockchains start speaking the same language? Interoperability breaks silos, allowing value, data, and smart contracts to move across networks.

Interoperability breaks down barriers, allowing value, data, and smart contracts to move freely across networks. This is how blockchain stops being a series of isolated experiments and becomes a unified, dynamic digital ecosystem, one that's bigger, smarter, and far more powerful than the sum of its parts.

The Problem of Silos

Most people outside this space still think of "the blockchain" as a single entity. In reality, there are thousands of independent networks, each with its own architecture, security model, and community. Bitcoin, Ethereum, Cardano, Polkadot, Stellar, Solana are all unique chains, often with limited ability to communicate with one another.

This is a bit like if we had dozens of disconnected mini-internets. Imagine needing a special browser and rules for every website. Early in the internet's history, that was actually the case. In the 1980s, local networks were walled off, universities and corporations ran their own systems that couldn't easily exchange data. It wasn't until standard protocols like TCP/IP unified them that the internet exploded into what we know today.

Blockchain is at a similar inflection point right now.

Without interoperability, each blockchain is like an island. Valuable data and assets are trapped. Smart contracts can only trigger actions inside their own ecosystem. Innovation is slowed by duplication of effort, as each chain tries to solve every problem on its own.

Interoperability solves this. It breaks down silos so networks can work together, pooling strengths, sharing resources, and opening the door to breakthroughs no single chain could achieve alone.

Why Interoperability Matters

Interoperability isn't just a technical convenience; it's a fundamental step in making blockchain reach its full potential. It means:

- **Assets can move across chains.** A token minted on Ethereum can be transferred to another chain where fees are lower or features are better, then brought back if needed.

- **Smart contracts can coordinate across systems.** For example, a contract on Solana could automatically execute a payment on Stellar or verify identity on Ethereum.

- Developers can build cross-chain applications that draw on the strengths of multiple blockchains, creating more powerful and user-friendly experiences.

It's like transforming a set of country roads into a vast highway system, where vehicles (data, assets, contracts) can travel quickly and reliably wherever they're needed.

Real-World Examples:

How Interoperability Is Already Changing the Game

- **Polkadot: Specialized Blockchains Connected by Design**
  Polkadot was created with interoperability as its core mission. It's a network of individual blockchains (called parachains) that connect through the Polkadot Relay Chain. This design means one chain can focus purely on privacy features, another on gaming, another on high-speed finance, and all of them can still communicate and share value securely. Instead of each blockchain trying to be a jack-of-all-trades, they can specialize and collaborate.
- **Quant: Building Bridges for Banks and Enterprises**
  Quant's Overledger is designed specifically to let different blockchains and even traditional banking systems talk to each other. Instead of requiring

companies to build separate systems for Ethereum, Hyperledger, or Ripple, Quant acts like an operating layer that connects them all.

For example, a bank could settle payments on one blockchain, store customer credentials on another, and manage regulatory compliance data on a third, all coordinated through Quant's technology. This kind of "network of networks" is what makes it possible for large institutions to adopt blockchain without being locked into a single ecosystem.

- **Cosmos: An Internet of Blockchains**
  Cosmos uses the Inter-Blockchain Communication (IBC) protocol to let different blockchains transfer assets and data. Think of it as a standardized language that any compatible chain can speak. This allows for seamless transactions and coordination, much like how your Gmail can talk to Yahoo or Outlook without a hitch. Projects ranging from decentralized exchanges to carbon credit platforms are already using Cosmos to bridge their operations.

- **Wrapped Tokens: The Bridge Before the Bridges**
  Before true interoperability protocols became widespread, the industry created workarounds. Wrapped tokens are one example. For instance, Wrapped Bitcoin (WBTC) is Bitcoin represented on

Ethereum. Bitcoin is locked in a secure system, and an equivalent amount of WBTC is minted on Ethereum. This allows Bitcoin holders to use their BTC in Ethereum-based DeFi apps. Earning yield, participating in lending, or securing loans without ever selling it.

- **Chainlink: Making Smart Contracts Smarter Across Chains**
  Chainlink started as an oracle network, feeding real-world data (like prices or weather) to smart contracts. But now it's pioneering cross-chain communication. Chainlink's Cross-Chain Interoperability Protocol (CCIP) aims to let smart contracts on different chains talk directly, unlocking things like decentralized insurance on one chain automatically triggering payouts on another.

The Bigger Opportunity: From Standalone Chains to an Interconnected World

Interoperability transforms blockchain from a scattered collection of tools into a coordinated digital economy.

- A retailer could track products on VeChain, settle invoices on Stellar, and ensure shipments on Ethereum without even knowing it's happening on different chains.

- A global workforce might get paid in local stablecoins on one blockchain, while their contracts are enforced on another, and reputation scores verified by a third.

- A single wallet app could let you hold and transact with assets from dozens of blockchains, finding the cheapest or fastest routes automatically similar to how your email client aggregates all your accounts into one place.

It's this seamless flow of value and data across systems that turns blockchain into a real foundation for the next internet.

Why This Matters for You

If you're an entrepreneur, interoperability means you can build applications that tap into multiple ecosystems at once bringing your ideas to a bigger market without being locked into a single chain's rules.

If you're an investor or builder, it means your assets can move where they're treated best. You aren't stuck with high fees or limited functionality because your token lives on a certain network.

If you care about fairness and resilience, interoperability means no single blockchain becomes too powerful or irreplaceable. Value and control are spread out, making the entire system healthier and more adaptable.

Key Takeaways

- Interoperability turns blockchains from isolated islands into an open, collaborative system where data, value, and contracts can move freely.

- Projects like Polkadot, Cosmos, Quant and Chainlink are laying the groundwork for a connected blockchain economy.

- Wrapped tokens have already shown demand for moving assets between chains, even before advanced protocols were ready.

- Interoperability means faster innovation, lower costs, and more choices, letting developers combine the best features of multiple chains.

- The promise of blockchain isn't truly realized until these networks can work together, unlocking a global digital marketplace.

Reflection Questions

1. Where in your industry or life could interconnected systems (rather than isolated platforms) create more efficiency or opportunity?

2. How might the ability for blockchains to communicate change your perspective on what's possible with decentralized technology?

3. What new products, services, or business models become feasible when data and money can move seamlessly across different networks?

4. In what ways does interoperability help protect against monopoly power or single points of failure in digital systems?

Chapter 8

Stablecoins Explained: Why the Biggest Financial Giants Are Making the Shift

Discover how stablecoins combine the speed of crypto with the stability of fiat as they reshape global payments, banking, and the future of money.

The Currency That Doesn't Crash at Midnight

Most people hardly carry cash anymore. A quick tap of a phone or swipe of a card and your coffee is paid for, your groceries are bagged, your ride is on its way. It feels instant. But behind the scenes, it's anything but.

Even when you pay for a coffee with Apple Pay or swipe a credit card at Target, the money doesn't actually move from your bank to the merchant right away. It's approved in seconds, but in reality, it can take one to three days to fully settle as it passes through multiple banks and payment processors, each taking a slice in fees.

Try sending money to a freelancer overseas or buying products from a supplier halfway around the world. Those transactions often take three to five days, can get stuck in manual compliance checks, and pile on hefty conversion fees.

Now imagine if there was a universal form of money that moved as quickly as cryptocurrency but held steady like the dollar. That's the power of stablecoins, and why the biggest banks and payment processors are not only paying attention but actively building and integrating them.

In the world of digital assets, where volatility often grabs the headlines, stablecoins offer something radically different: predictability. They're designed to keep a steady value, typically pegged to a fiat currency like the US dollar or euro. This blend of digital speed and fiat stability is beginning to transform how businesses, banks, and individuals exchange value across the globe.

What Are Stablecoins?

At their core, stablecoins are digital tokens that live on a blockchain but mirror the value of traditional currencies. They aim to combine the best of both worlds:

- The instantaneous settlement, global reach, and programmable features of cryptocurrency

- The price reliability of fiat money

Most stablecoins achieve this by being "backed" by real-world assets. For example, each USDC or USDT token is supposed to be matched by a corresponding dollar (or equivalent reserves) held in a bank account.

But the stability mechanism can vary:

- **Fiat-collateralized stablecoins:** Backed by cash or cash equivalents held in reserve. Examples include USDC (by Circle and Coinbase) and RLUSD (by Ripple).

- **Crypto-collateralized stablecoins:** Backed by other cryptocurrencies, often with overcollateralization to handle market swings. DAI by MakerDAO is a leading example.

- **Algorithmic stablecoins:** Use smart contracts to adjust supply and demand automatically, maintaining their peg without traditional reserves. These are riskier and have faced challenges, as seen with Terra's UST collapse.

Why Stablecoins Matter in the Big Picture

Stablecoins aren't simply a clever tool for crypto traders to park funds. They represent a fundamental evolution in money, bridging the worlds of blockchain and traditional finance in a way few other innovations can.

They solve three major problems:

- **Volatility:** Unlike Bitcoin or Ethereum, stablecoins are designed not to swing wildly in price, making them useful for everyday transactions and financial contracts.

- **Speed and cost:** Stablecoin transfers settle in minutes, not days, without the high fees of wire transfers or credit cards.

- **Global accessibility:** Anyone with a smartphone and internet connection can send or receive stablecoins, by passing traditional banking barriers.

This is why multinational corporations and financial giants are not just watching stablecoins, they're building on them.

Major Players Getting on Board

Visa and Mastercard

Visa has piloted programs to settle payments using USDC on the Ethereum blockchain, cutting out traditional correspondent banking steps. Mastercard is developing tools to support stablecoin payments across its vast merchant network. These moves are strategic bets on faster, cheaper, programmable money.

JPMorgan

JPMorgan created its own internal stablecoin called JPM Coin to move billions across its institutional client accounts. Unlike public stablecoins, JPM Coin is private and permissioned, = demonstrating how even the world's largest banks see value in blockchain-based settlement.

PayPal

In 2023, PayPal launched its own dollar-backed stablecoin, PYUSD, aimed at simplifying crypto-to-fiat conversions and broadening the digital payments landscape. This brings stablecoins into the wallets of millions of existing PayPal customers.

AWS

Amazon Web Services is not creating stablecoins itself, but it provides the critical cloud infrastructure that powers many of the world's largest stablecoin ecosystems. From running Ethereum and Hyperledger nodes to hosting Circle's USDC operations and supporting banks integrating Ripple's XRP Ledger, AWS is quietly becoming the backbone for how stablecoins and blockchain networks scale. This makes AWS a hidden force behind the shift toward instant, global, blockchain-based settlement.

Governments and Central Banks

Many central banks are studying or piloting their own stablecoin-like instruments, known as central bank digital currencies (CBDCs), while a growing number, including the Bahamas, Nigeria, and Jamaica have already fully launched them. China's digital yuan is even further along, operating large-scale trials across dozens of cities with millions of citizens actively using it for payments, transit, and retail purchases. Though CBDCs differ from decentralized stablecoins, they share the same goal: blending digital speed with fiat reliability.

How CBDCs Differ from Stablecoins

Though they can look similar on the surface, CBDCs and stablecoins are fundamentally different. A CBDC is a direct liability of a central bank, essentially just the country's official currency in digital form, controlled entirely by the state. A stablecoin, on the other hand, is typically issued by a private company or protocol, pegged to a fiat currency, and circulates on public or semi-public blockchains. Both aim to combine digital speed with fiat stability, but one is a government tool, the other a private or decentralized alternative.

How Stablecoins Are Being Used Today

Remittances and Cross-Border Payments

Traditional international money transfers are slow and costly. A single payment might pass through five intermediaries, each taking a cut. Stablecoins allow someone in the U.S. to send funds directly to a family member in the Philippines, who can receive it almost instantly, often with near-zero fees.

DeFi and Yield Opportunities

Stablecoins power much of decentralized finance. People deposit USDC or DAI into protocols like Aave or Compound to earn interest, provide liquidity, or use them as collateral for loans. This creates entirely new financial markets that run 24/7, without banks.

Protecting Wealth in Volatile Economies

In countries experiencing hyperinflation, citizens turn to stablecoins to preserve value. A business owner in Argentina might keep profits in USDT to avoid local currency depreciation, giving them financial tools once reserved for international corporations.

E-Commerce and Payroll

Companies are starting to pay international contractors with stablecoins, sidestepping wire fees and currency headaches. Merchants are exploring stablecoin checkout options, offering customers global payment methods that settle faster than credit cards.

The Bigger Economic Shift

Stablecoins are not merely a side story in crypto, they are becoming foundational infrastructure for a new kind of global economy. They act like digital glue, holding together traditional banks, blockchain networks, and everyday users in a seamless web of value exchange.

Think of them as the oil in the engine of decentralized finance: not flashy, but absolutely essential. They grease the wheels of payments, contracts, and applications that rely on blockchain's speed and transparency without inheriting its volatility.

Real-World Examples: Stablecoins in Action

- **Circle's USDC:** Used by thousands of fintech apps, from neobanks to lending platforms. It's audited monthly for reserves, which builds trust among institutional partners.

- **DAI:** MakerDAO's decentralized stablecoin is managed entirely by smart contracts and community governance, pioneering trustless stability.

- **Tether (USDT):** The most traded stablecoin globally, critical for liquidity across crypto exchanges. Despite controversy over its reserve disclosures, it dominates volume.

- **PayPal's PYUSD:** Gives mainstream consumers an easy gateway to stablecoins without needing to set up separate wallets.

STABLECOIN

FIAT
STABILITY

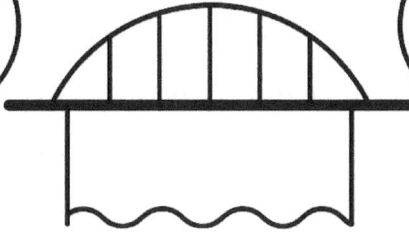

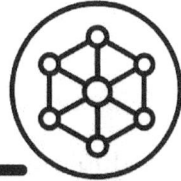

CRYPTOCURRENCY
SPEED

**A BRIDGE BETWEEN
CRYPTO SPEED AND
FIAT STABILITY**

Key Takeaways

- Stablecoins blend the speed and global reach of cryptocurrency with the steady value of fiat money, solving problems that neither can address alone.

- Major players like Visa, JPMorgan, and PayPal are adopting stablecoins to streamline payments, reduce costs, and create programmable money.

- Stablecoins enable everything from instant cross-border payments to decentralized finance, reshaping how individuals and businesses manage money.

- Far from speculative assets, stablecoins are quietly becoming the backbone of a new global financial system.

Reflection Questions

1. How might stablecoins change the way you think about sending, saving, or investing money?

2. What traditional fees or delays in your business or personal finances could stablecoins help eliminate?

3. In what ways could stablecoins empower people in unstable economies or underbanked regions?

4. How does the idea of programmable money, transactions that execute automatically under certain conditions, open new possibilities for how you work or invest?

5. What could happen if major governments and corporations increasingly adopt stablecoins or their own digital currencies?

Part 2

Real-World Applications and Human Empowerment

How blockchain is already changing lives, industries, and identity.

Chapter 9

How Blockchain Is Reinventing Digital Trust

Explore how blockchain is increasing security, reducing fraud, and restoring trust through tamper-proof records and decentralized systems.

Why Trust Has Become Fragile

Everyday life depends on trust, often in ways we don't see.

When you deposit money in the bank, buy groceries online, visit the doctor, or sign a contract, you're placing trust in systems to work properly, securely, and fairly.
You're trusting that:

- The bank won't misuse your money or accidentally lose your balance.

- The e-commerce site won't steal your credit card data.

- Medical records will remain private and unchanged.

- A signed agreement will be honored, and that if it's not, there's a clear record of what was agreed.

For most of modern history, this kind of trust was managed by centralized institutions, banks, corporations, governments, and legal systems.

They built their business models around being trustworthy intermediaries.
But time and again, these systems have failed.

- **Massive data breaches** companies exposing sensitive information of hundreds of millions of people.

- **Companies creating fake customer accounts** to meet sales targets.

- **Hospitals accidentally (or maliciously) changing patient records** or losing them altogether.

- **Global supply chains riddled with counterfeit goods**, often undetected until harm is done.

What all of these have in common is that trust rested in the hands of a few.

When those hands were careless, greedy, or dishonest, trust collapsed, and there was little the average person could do.

How Blockchain Reimagines Trust

Blockchain introduces a completely different approach.

Instead of requiring us to trust a single institution to keep honest records, protect data, and honor agreements, blockchain distributes trust across thousands of independent computers around the world.

This creates what some call "trustless trust."

It doesn't mean there's no trust, it means you no longer have to place blind trust in a middleman. Trust is baked into the system itself through:

- **Decentralization:** Data isn't stored on one company's servers. It lives on thousands of computers (nodes) simultaneously. No single party can change it without everyone knowing.

- **Immutability:** Once a transaction or record is added, it's cryptographically linked to the blocks before it. Changing even a tiny detail would require rewriting every block across the entire network, a practical impossibility.

- **Transparency:** Most blockchains are public. Anyone can view the records. This doesn't mean everyone can see your private data, but they can see transactions, making manipulation nearly impossible to hide.

In short: trust is enforced by code and math, not by promises or private ledgers.

Why This Matters More Than Ever

In the old model, trust could be quietly broken behind closed doors.
An accountant could fudge books. A data manager could secretly sell private files. A warehouse could swap real products for fakes.

The average person would never know, until it was too late.

With blockchain, records aren't controlled by a private database that can be quietly altered. They're recorded on a chain that's visible, permanent, and verified by consensus.

This means:

- Auditors no longer just trust companies' reports, they can cryptographically verify them.

- Governments can't secretly rewrite public records without global detection.

- Hospitals can't accidentally mix up or alter medical histories without instantly breaking the cryptographic chain.

This is revolutionary. It's shifting trust from fragile human systems to a system of provable integrity.

How Blockchain Strengthens Security

Think about how most data is stored today.
Your bank records, insurance details, property titles, and medical files are all sitting on servers controlled by individual companies.

If a hacker breaks into that server, they can steal, alter, or destroy records.

If an insider wants to commit fraud, they often can without anyone knowing until after damage is done.

Blockchain flips this.

- **No single point of failure:** Because the data is distributed, there is no master vault to break into. A hacker would need to simultaneously compromise thousands of independent computers.

- **Cryptographic signatures:** Every transaction is signed with digital keys, ensuring authenticity. If someone tries to forge a transaction, the network rejects it automatically.

- **Built-in validation:** Changes only happen when the network reaches consensus. One rogue actor can't push through an unauthorized change.

For example:

- In traditional accounting, fraud might go undetected for years until an audit finds discrepancies.

- On a blockchain-based ledger, even minor inconsistencies would instantly break the chain, revealing tampering immediately.

Reducing Fraud and Costly Errors

Blockchain is already being applied to cut fraud and reduce costly mistakes.

Supply Chains

- Luxury brands are using blockchain to track goods from raw materials to finished products. This makes it nearly impossible for counterfeit items to be swapped in without detection.

- Walmart uses blockchain to track food from farms to shelves, improving safety and reducing recalls.

Insurance

- Smart contracts on blockchain can automatically verify claims against a shared ledger of policies, reducing false claims and disputes.

Banking

- Many banks are moving to blockchain-based reconciliation systems, which automatically match transactions across institutions, eliminating manual errors and fraud.

By automating verification and keeping an unchangeable audit trail, blockchain minimizes the room for deception.

Restoring Broken Trust Through Decentralization

This is perhaps the most profound change.

In centralized systems, power concentrates.
A handful of tech giants decide what data is real. A few global banks control capital flows. Governments maintain huge databases they can edit at will.

Blockchain decentralizes this power.

- Your identity can be anchored to a blockchain wallet that only you control.

- Transactions can be verified by global networks, not by a single company.

- Rules can be enforced by smart contracts that execute automatically, without needing lawyers or banks to approve every step.

For example:

- Instead of trusting a centralized credit bureau to fairly report your history, future systems could use blockchain-based proofs that you control and share selectively.

- Instead of needing to trust a land office to honor your property deed, your ownership could be permanently recorded on a blockchain, viewable and provable by anyone.

This doesn't just reduce fraud, it rebalances power, putting individuals back at the center of their own data and transactions.

Real-World Examples: Blockchain in Action

- Estonia anchors its entire e-government system to blockchain. Citizen records are protected from tampering and auditable by design.

- IBM and Maersk's TradeLens uses blockchain to track global shipping containers, reducing paperwork fraud and customs delays.

- Provenance platforms in fashion and wine use blockchain to certify authenticity, fighting multi-billion-dollar counterfeit markets.

- Major auditing firms use blockchain-based ledgers to create instantly verifiable accounting trails, dramatically cutting the time and uncertainty in financial audits.

Even more quietly, thousands of companies are embedding blockchain for internal compliance and security, protecting data in ways traditional databases simply can't.

Key Takeaways

- Traditional trust depends on human institutions, banks, companies, regulators, which can fail, lie, or get hacked.

- Blockchain rebuilds trust from the ground up through decentralization, cryptography, and transparent ledgers.

- This shifts trust from fragile promises to verifiable systems. Instead of "trust us," it's "verify yourself anytime."

- As industries integrate blockchain, they're not just adopting new tech, they're laying foundations for a more transparent, fraud-resistant, user-empowered world.

Reflection Questions

1. Think of an industry where trust has repeatedly been broken. How might blockchain change it?

2. How would knowing your records can't be secretly altered change your confidence in institutions?

3. In what areas of your personal or business life would you feel safer with blockchain-based systems?

4. What concerns might you still have, even with blockchain, about privacy, control, or power shifts?

Chapter 10

How Blockchain Is Securing Your Digital Identity (And Why It Matters)

In a world where data is currency, blockchain offers a way to reclaim, protect, and control your digital identity.

The New Currency of Trust

Trust used to be local. People knew who farmed their food, who sewed their clothes, and who they were trading with at the local market. Business was personal and reputation was earned face to face. As societies scaled, that trust shifted to institutions. Banks, governments, corporations, and centralized platforms took on the role of intermediaries, guaranteeing that money moved as promised, property changed hands properly, and agreements were enforced.

In many ways, this system worked remarkably well. Global trade flourished. Millions of people could buy homes, build companies, and transact with strangers across oceans. But over time, cracks appeared. Massive data breaches exposed personal information. Corruption and opaque accounting scandals shattered confidence. Centralized platforms censored or distorted information. In short, many of the institutions meant to safeguard trust proved they could fail or abuse their power.

Today, trust itself has become one of the most fragile commodities in the digital age. As more of life moved online, verifying what is true and who is trustworthy has grown increasingly complex. From manipulated news to fraudulent transactions and deep-fake videos, the modern world faces a profound crisis of credibility. Blockchain is emerging as a powerful remedy to this crisis, not by replacing trust, but by radically restructuring how it is established, maintained, and verified.

Why Traditional Digital Trust Is Broken

The internet we use today was never built with trust in mind. It was designed to move information quickly, not necessarily to prove its authenticity or secure its ownership. The core systems of the web still function by copying and transmitting data. When you send an email or share a photo, you do not transfer the original, you duplicate it. That is why digital files can be easily altered, forged, or stolen.

For decades, trust online depended on central authorities to stand in the gap. We trust banks like Wells Fargo, Citibank, and HSBC to update ledgers accurately. We trust social media platforms like Facebook and TikTok to handle our identities and content responsibly. We trust corporations like Equifax or Marriott to secure customer records. Yet history is full of examples showing how these systems can be hacked, corrupted, or manipulated. Millions have had personal data exposed in breaches at companies such as Yahoo or Target. Fake reviews distort online marketplaces on platforms like Amazon. Fraudulent invoices slip through global supply chains. Even elections around the world have suffered from misinformation campaigns designed to sway outcomes.

In this environment, traditional trust models feel increasingly brittle. People want new ways to be certain that what they see is authentic, that transactions actually occurred, and that records cannot be secretly changed later. Blockchain provides a fresh foundation for building that kind of trust at scale.

How Blockchain Creates Trust Without Middlemen

At its core, blockchain is a shared database that is publicly accessible, cryptographically secured, and chronologically ordered. Instead of relying on one company, government, or server to manage data, a blockchain distributes copies of the same ledger across thousands of independent computers, called nodes. Every time new data is added, it must be verified by the network through mathematical rules, then permanently recorded. Each new entry links to the one before it, creating a chain of transparent, tamper-evident records.

This architecture means two powerful things. First, no single party can quietly rewrite history. To alter past data, someone would have to convince a majority of the network to approve the change, which is practically impossible on large, well-secured blockchains like Bitcoin or Ethereum. Second, anyone can independently verify what is recorded. They do not have to trust a private company's internal database or take a website's word for it. They can look directly at the blockchain itself.

Because of these properties, blockchain transforms the question from "Do I trust this company or platform?" into "Can I verify this data myself?" This shift from trusting institutions to trusting code and open networks is at the heart of why blockchain is being called a new foundation for digital trust.

Real-World Examples of Blockchain Trust in Action

Preventing Counterfeit Products

Luxury brands such as Louis Vuitton, Prada, and Cartier have long battled fakes. Shoppers buying high-end watches, handbags, or sneakers online often have no easy way to confirm authenticity. Blockchain changes that by linking each product to a unique digital record from the point of manufacture. The Aura Blockchain Consortium, formed by LVMH, Prada Group, and Cartier, is already using blockchain-powered certificates that consumers can scan with a phone to confirm origin, ownership, and even repair history.

Supply Chain Verification

Food fraud is another costly problem. Supermarkets might label fish as sustainably caught when it is not. Meat could come from unsafe facilities. By recording every step on a blockchain from farm to processor to grocery shelf, businesses create a transparent audit trail. Walmart, in partnership with IBM's Food Trust blockchain platform, has piloted systems that let customers trace mangos or pork all the way back to the farm. If there is ever a contamination scare, blockchain records make it faster to find and fix.

Proving Identity and Credentials

Blockchain is also being used to protect people's identities. Instead of trusting tech giants like Google or Meta with personal data, individuals can hold verifiable digital credentials in their own wallets. Massachusetts Institute of Technology issues blockchain-secured diplomas that employers can instantly validate without needing to call a registrar. Estonia has pioneered a national ID system tied to blockchain that gives its citizens direct control over their data and digital signatures.

Securing Financial Records

Traditional financial ledgers can be altered behind closed doors. Blockchain systems like those used by decentralized finance platforms such as Compound and Aave publish every transaction on a public ledger. That does not mean personal details are exposed, but the flow of money is open for all to see. This transparency discourages fraud and gives regulators and customers alike a more trustworthy window into financial activity.

How Blockchain Reduces Fraud and Human Error

Blockchain minimizes many of the risks tied to human manipulation or clerical mistakes. Since records are confirmed by multiple parties before being added and cannot be quietly edited later, it becomes nearly impossible for someone to cook the books or sneak in unauthorized changes.

Imagine a global shipping firm like Maersk, where dozens of subcontractors update delivery logs. In a traditional system, a dishonest worker could adjust timestamps to hide delays or reroute goods improperly. With blockchain, each update is signed, time-stamped, and visible to all authorized parties. Trying to alter data after the fact would immediately break the chain's cryptographic links, raising red flags.

Similarly, in digital advertising, fraud is rampant because middlemen report metrics privately. Unilever and Nestlé have tested blockchain systems to track ad spending, letting advertisers see exactly how and where their money was spent, reducing billions lost annually to fake clicks and bots.

Trust in an Era of Deepfakes and AI

As artificial intelligence grows more advanced, so does its ability to create convincing fakes. A video can show a politician saying things they never said. A photo can depict events that never happened. This makes blockchain's role in trust even more crucial.

Reuters and The New York Times are experimenting with blockchain projects to timestamp and certify the origin of legitimate photos, videos, and documents. For example, a news agency could upload a video to a blockchain at the moment of recording. Later, anyone could compare a suspicious clip circulating online with the original blockchain record to spot alterations.

This kind of verifiable media chain could become essential in the fight against misinformation, protecting elections, reputations, and public confidence in an age where seeing is no longer believing.

Building Trust in Peer-to-Peer Economies

Blockchain also enables people to transact directly without relying on giant platforms that charge fees and hold data. On marketplaces built on smart contracts, two strangers can exchange assets knowing the contract will execute exactly as programmed, automatically enforcing rules. Payments only complete once conditions are met. This creates a new kind of trust that does not depend on personal relationships or third-party guarantees.

Decentralized rental platforms like Dtravel are exploring this concept. Imagine renting a car from a stranger through a blockchain-based app. The smart contract could ensure that payment, insurance verification, and even temporary digital keys all happen automatically and transparently.

Why This Matters Now

We are living through a crisis of trust, not just in technology but in institutions broadly. Studies from Edelman's Trust Barometer show public faith in banks, media outlets, and governments has fallen dramatically over the past decade. People want systems where trust is built in by design, not demanded through reputation alone.

Blockchain does not solve every problem, but it offers a radically different architecture. By shifting trust from opaque systems to open, verifiable records, it provides a toolkit for restoring confidence in a wide range of interactions, from banking to news to everyday contracts.

Key Takeaways

• Blockchain turns trust from a matter of blind faith into a matter of transparent verification

• It protects records from tampering and reduces the chance of fraud or human error

• It gives individuals, businesses, and regulators an open ledger to confirm what really happened

• In a world where misinformation and data breaches are rampant, blockchain provides a new foundation for credibility

---

Reflection Questions

1. How might blockchain change the way you think about trusting businesses, media, or financial systems?

2. What processes in your work or life could benefit from tamper-proof records?

3. Where have you had to trust institutions that later failed or disappointed you, and how could blockchain have changed the outcome?

SECURING YOUR DIGITAL IDENTITY

- **OWNERSHIP & CONTROL**
- **PROTECTION FROM THEFT**
- **PRIVACY OF DATA**

Chapter 11

Fighting Misinformation and Deepfakes

Blockchain is being used to verify truth in a digital world flooded with fake news, AI-generated content, and manipulated media. Restoring trust through transparency and secure provenance.

The Crisis of Truth in a Digital World

In the early days of the internet, it was revolutionary simply to publish ideas online. Most information still carried the weight of its offline source. News stories came from recognizable outlets. Photos and videos were difficult and costly to fake at scale. Trust was easier to maintain because manipulation was harder.

That world is gone. Today, anyone can publish anything to a global audience instantly. Platforms like YouTube, TikTok, and Instagram have turned every user into a broadcaster. Meanwhile, social media algorithms push sensational content, whether true or not, because outrage and shock drive engagement.

The problem is no longer that information is hard to find. It is that the internet is drowning in too much of it, with no reliable filter for truth. This has opened the door for:

- Fake news stories designed to mislead voters or inflame social divisions.

- AI-generated articles and websites that churn out plausible but entirely fabricated reports.

- Deepfake videos showing public figures saying or doing things they never did.

- Doctored photos that spread faster than corrections ever could.

It is already destabilizing societies, financial markets, and individual lives.

During the 2016 US election, viral falsehoods about candidates spread more widely than factual reporting. In 2022, a deepfake of Ukrainian President Volodymyr Zelensky appeared online, telling troops to surrender, seeking to demoralize a nation under attack. Fraudulent press releases have caused companies' stock prices to swing billions in minutes before the truth emerged.

The digital age has democratized publishing but also democratized deception.

Why Current Systems Fail to Stop It

Much of today's internet runs on models designed for speed and scale, not for verifying authenticity. Social media companies rely on after-the-fact content moderation, which is slow, unevenly applied, and easily circumvented by new accounts or shifting narratives.

Fact-checkers are overwhelmed by the volume of new content. By the time a false story is debunked, millions may have seen and believed it. Worse, corrections rarely travel as far or as fast as the original lie.

Traditional publishers once served as gatekeepers of credibility. But in an era where blogs, influencers, and anonymous accounts can reach audiences larger than newspapers ever did, those old barriers are gone.

Financial incentives make it even harder. Clicks and ad revenue reward viral stories, not accurate ones. A fabricated headline can earn money long before a retraction cuts off its spread.

This leaves a glaring question. If content can be created and distributed globally in seconds, how do we prove what is real?

How Blockchain Changes the Verification Game

Blockchain brings a radically different architecture for establishing trust. Instead of relying on intermediaries or trying to fact-check an endless flood of data, it builds trust into the system at the moment of creation.

A blockchain is a distributed ledger. Once a piece of data, whether a photo, a video, a document, or a transaction, is recorded, it is time-stamped, cryptographically sealed, and linked to the previous record. It becomes nearly impossible to alter without detection.

This means blockchain can serve as a transparent, tamper-proof history of digital content. It does not prevent someone from posting a fake image. But it makes it easy to verify whether that image originated from a trusted source and if it has been altered since.

Imagine watching a video clip of a world leader making a shocking statement. On today's internet, there is often no easy way to know if it is authentic. With blockchain provenance, that same video could carry an embedded cryptographic proof of origin. Anyone could instantly check the blockchain to see who published it, when, and whether it matches the original file.

This flips the burden. Instead of asking viewers to decide if something feels real, content can prove itself.

Real-World Examples of Blockchain Battling Misinformation

Leading news organizations, tech companies, and nonprofits are actively building systems to verify content integrity using blockchain.

The New York Times and Project Origin

The New York Times launched an experiment called The News Provenance Project. It uses blockchain to store metadata about images when and where a photo was taken, who published it, and whether it was edited. This creates an unalterable record that travels with the image wherever it goes online.

Similarly, Project Origin, backed by the BBC, Microsoft, CBC Radio-Canada, and the New York Times, is creating standards for attaching cryptographic provenance data to content at the point of creation. This way, when viewers see a video or photo, they can instantly verify its authenticity.

Reuters and the Content Authenticity Initiative

Reuters is part of the Content Authenticity Initiative, alongside Adobe and Twitter, which embeds secure metadata into images and videos. Blockchain can store and verify these records so anyone can confirm the history of a piece of content.

Blockchain for Election Integrity

In countries facing misinformation campaigns designed to sway elections, startups are using blockchain to log official statements and press releases. This ensures that forged or altered versions can be easily debunked by comparing them to the original blockchain entry.

For example, Civic Ledger in Australia has explored using blockchain to secure election data and public records. This builds a chain of trust for statements and documents critical to democratic processes.

Combatting Counterfeit Certifications and Diplomas

Fake degrees are another rampant problem. Universities such as MIT and the University of Bahrain issue blockchain-based diplomas that employers can instantly verify. This cuts out fraudulent credentials, which are often used to secure jobs or visas.

AI, Deepfakes, and the Next Frontier

Artificial intelligence is rapidly increasing the sophistication of fakes. Tools like DALL-E and Midjourney can create photorealistic images from text prompts. Voice cloning can replicate a person's speech with frightening accuracy. Deepfake video tools can swap faces or alter speech to create entirely false scenarios.

Blockchain is emerging as a vital counterweight. By registering legitimate media on a public ledger, it creates a reference point. Even if fake videos circulate, viewers can check them against the blockchain record to confirm whether they match the original.

Several blockchain startups are now specializing in digital watermarking and forensic analysis, logging signatures of authentic content so manipulation can be detected.

This is becoming essential not only for journalism and elections but also for companies. A single deepfake video could tank a company's stock or spread damaging false claims about executives. Blockchain-secured proofs offer a way to safeguard reputations and market stability.

Building a Future of Verifiable Media

Imagine a near future where every important photo, document, or piece of video evidence comes with a blockchain-anchored certificate of authenticity. Instead of relying on gut feelings or fragmented fact-checks, people could run a quick verification scan.

For businesses, this means contracts, invoices, and supply chain records that prove their own validity. For governments, it could mean tamper-proof public statements or certified election data. For individuals, it means resumes, portfolios, or even social posts that carry cryptographic signatures showing they are genuine.

This does not eliminate deception entirely. But it raises the cost and difficulty of faking content. It gives truth a technological advantage.

Key Takeaways

• The internet is flooded with fake news, AI-generated articles, and deepfake videos that erode trust

• Traditional methods of policing content rely on human moderation, which is slow and often fails to keep up

• Blockchain offers a new foundation by recording the origin and history of digital content on tamper-proof ledgers

• Major companies like the New York Times, BBC, Reuters, and Adobe are using blockchain to secure media integrity

• As deepfakes and synthetic media grow more advanced, blockchain will become a critical tool to defend truth and maintain public confidence

---

Reflection Questions

1. How might blockchain-verified content change the way you decide what news or videos to trust?

2. In your work or personal life, where could having a provable record of authenticity protect you from fraud or reputational harm?

3. What are the potential risks or challenges of tying so much credibility to a blockchain system?

4. How could this shift influence social media platforms and the spread of viral content in the next decade?

Chapter 12

Behind the Barcode: How Blockchain Tracks What You Buy

See how blockchain is transforming supply chains by tracking products from origin to shelf, increasing transparency and trust for consumers.

Why Trust in Supply Chains is Broken

Every time you pick up a product from a store shelf, there is an invisible story behind it. Where were the tomatoes in that jar of salsa grown? Was the leather in your handbag sourced responsibly? Is the medication in your cabinet exactly what it says on the label?

Most people assume that the items they buy are authentic, safe, and ethically produced. Yet behind many barcodes lies a murky, complex journey that is difficult to trace. Global supply chains stretch across continents, involving dozens of intermediaries, farmers, manufacturers, brokers, shipping companies, distributors, and retailers. Each one updates records in its own systems, often with little standardization or oversight.

This creates an environment where:

- Counterfeit goods can slip in unnoticed

- Ethical certifications may be forged or applied inconsistently

- Contaminated or defective products can go undetected for too long

Consumers pay the price. Brands lose credibility. Regulators struggle to enforce standards. The traditional supply chain model has simply not kept pace with the modern demand for transparency.

How Big the Problem Really Is

Consider these staggering realities. The World Health Organization estimates that one in ten medical products in low and middle-income countries is substandard or outright fake. The Organization for Economic Co-operation and Development reports the global trade in counterfeit goods is worth over $500 billion each year, infiltrating everything from luxury handbags to airplane parts.

In the food industry, contamination scares are all too common. In 2022, a bacterial contamination at Abbott Nutrition's plant, one of the largest infant formula producers in the United States, led to massive recalls and left store shelves empty across the country. Because traditional supply chain records were scattered across manufacturers, distributors, and retailers, it took weeks to determine the full scope of the problem. Parents struggled to find safe formula, often with no clear way to know if the product they held was from an affected batch. Hospitals and clinics faced shortages that put vulnerable infants at risk. The absence of unified, tamper-proof tracking turned what could have been a targeted response into a nationwide crisis that deeply eroded public trust.

Consumers want more than assurances. They want proof.

How Blockchain Reinvents Product Traceability

Blockchain is changing the equation by creating a single, tamper-resistant source of truth that can be shared by everyone in the supply chain. Instead of each participant keeping siloed databases, blockchain connects the entire journey of a product on one distributed ledger. Each time an item moves or changes hands, that event is recorded, time-stamped, and secured by cryptographic principles.

This offers several transformative benefits:

- **End-to-end visibility:** Every step, from raw material extraction to final sale, is recorded and viewable.

- **Tamper resistance:** Once data is added, it cannot be secretly changed. Attempts to alter records are immediately evident.

- **Real-time auditing:** Brands and regulators can monitor supply chains continuously instead of relying on periodic paper audits.

- **Consumer trust:** Shoppers can scan a QR code and see verified details about where and how a product was made.

With blockchain, the barcode becomes more than a price lookup. It becomes a passport of authenticity and ethical sourcing.

Real-World Examples of Blockchain in Supply Chains

Tracking Food from Farm to Fork

Walmart, one of the world's largest retailers, has partnered with IBM's Food Trust blockchain platform to improve food safety. Before using blockchain, it took Walmart nearly seven days to trace a package of sliced mangoes back to the farm. With blockchain, it takes just over two seconds. This means if there is a contamination issue, Walmart can rapidly identify the specific source and remove only affected batches, protecting consumers and avoiding needless waste.

Nestlé and Carrefour have also used blockchain to let customers trace milk, baby formula, and even free-range chicken back to farms, building confidence that product claims are genuine.

Authenticating Luxury Goods

Counterfeiting is a multi-billion-dollar problem for luxury brands. LVMH, the parent company of Louis Vuitton, Tiffany & Co, Prada, Cartier, and Dior, co-founded the Aura Blockchain

Consortium. This platform records details of luxury items on blockchain, so customers can verify authenticity and ownership history. When someone buys a handbag or watch, they can scan a digital certificate linked to blockchain, proving it is not a sophisticated fake.

Aura Consortium's Private Blockchain Approach

Aura Blockchain Consortium operates differently than typical public blockchain projects. As a private group formed by leading luxury houses, it does not issue a token because its members collectively run the network to secure product data. By using a permissioned blockchain, they maintain strict control over who can validate transactions, which helps protect proprietary details about their goods. Even so, Aura ties its records to Ethereum by anchoring them periodically, adding an extra layer of transparency and leveraging Ethereum's immutability without incurring constant gas fees for every transaction. This hybrid approach allows them to assure customers of authenticity while avoiding the volatility and public congestion of fully token-driven systems.

Ethical Diamonds and Minerals

De Beers, the world's largest diamond producer, has developed Tracr, a blockchain system that tracks diamonds from mines to retail stores. Each stone's unique attributes are logged on blockchain, ensuring it was sourced from conflict-free areas and processed responsibly. This is particularly powerful in an industry long plagued by "blood diamonds."

Similarly, Volkswagen and Ford have tested blockchain solutions to trace cobalt used in electric vehicle batteries, ensuring it comes from mines that meet labor and environmental standards.

Preventing Fraud and Reducing Recalls

Traditional supply chain records are vulnerable to fraud. Unscrupulous suppliers might mislabel products to secure higher prices. For example, fish can be swapped for cheaper species or falsely branded as sustainably caught.

Blockchain's transparency makes this type of deception far harder. Once a shipment is recorded, each new handoff updates the chain. If someone tries to change data, say, to upgrade the origin of shrimp from a questionable source to a certified one, the alteration would not match previous records, immediately triggering alerts.

Norwegian seafood giant Kvarøy Arctic uses IBM blockchain technology to track salmon from farm to fork, reassuring chefs and diners that their fish meets premium standards.

When problems do occur, blockchain makes it easier to pinpoint issues. Instead of recalling entire product lines, companies can isolate only the affected batches. This precision saves money, protects brand reputation, and reduces panic.

VeChain's Public Blockchain for Mass Transparency

While many high-profile supply chain solutions are built on private or consortium blockchains, VeChain has taken a different path by developing one of the largest public blockchains dedicated to supply chain and asset tracking. VeChain partners with major enterprises like Walmart China, Bayer, BMW, and PwC to create permanent, tamper-resistant records that track goods across global networks. Walmart China, for instance, uses VeChain to trace fresh foods, allowing customers to scan QR codes and see farm-to-shelf details. In pharmaceuticals, Bayer is piloting systems on VeChain to verify clinical data and drug movement, reducing the risk of counterfeit medicine.

Unlike private systems that hide data from public view, VeChain's architecture makes these records available on a decentralized ledger. It uses a two-token model: VET as the main value carrier and VTHO to pay for transactions, similar to how Ethereum uses Ether for gas. However, VeChain's design keeps costs stable, making it attractive for companies needing predictable transaction fees on high-volume supply chains. By anchoring trust in a transparent, widely accessible network, VeChain demonstrates how blockchain can secure global commerce at scale, beyond luxury items or confined pilots. It pushes the promise of visible, verifiable supply chains into everyday retail and healthcare, turning what was once hidden into something provable by anyone, anywhere.

Bringing Transparency to Everyday Purchases

For consumers, blockchain turns trust from blind faith into informed choice. A shopper can scan a QR code on a chocolate bar and see proof it was made with ethically sourced cocoa. A parent buying baby formula can verify that it was manufactured in certified facilities with documented safety checks.

This is not a distant future. Carrefour, one of Europe's largest supermarket chains, uses blockchain to provide traceability for dozens of products. Customers shopping for free-range chicken, eggs, or cheese can view the entire production story down to the farm and feed lot.

It also supports growing demands for sustainability. Shoppers concerned about deforestation or carbon impact can see verified records showing how goods were produced and transported.

Beyond Products: Securing Logistics and Paperwork

Blockchain is not just about tracking the goods themselves. It is also transforming the labyrinth of paperwork that moves alongside physical items. International shipping involves bills of lading, customs declarations, and compliance certificates that often pass through many hands, increasing risk of error or forgery.

Streamlining Compliance and Trade with GSBN

The Global Shipping Business Network (GSBN) is showing how blockchain can simplify this complexity on a massive scale. Based in Hong Kong, GSBN is a not-for-profit consortium that includes major players like COSCO Shipping, Hapag-Lloyd, and PSA International. By connecting carriers, port operators, and logistics companies on a secure blockchain, GSBN enables critical shipping data to be shared in near real time. This transparency streamlines customs clearances, reduces paperwork mistakes, and accelerates the flow of containers across borders. As more ports and trade hubs join the network, GSBN demonstrates how decentralized, tamper-resistant ledgers can cut costs, increase accountability, and build trust in global trade.

Key Takeaways

• Blockchain turns barcodes into gateways for transparency, tracking a product's journey from origin to consumer

• Major companies like Walmart, LVMH, and De Beers use blockchain to improve safety, fight counterfeits, and prove ethical sourcing

• With tamper-resistant records, fraud becomes harder, recalls become faster and more targeted, and consumers can shop with greater confidence

• Blockchain supply chains support new demands for sustainability and fair trade, offering proof instead of promises

---

Reflection Questions

1. How would knowing exactly where and how products were made change your shopping habits?

2. In what industries that you interact with would blockchain transparency have the biggest impact?

3. What concerns might arise if this level of tracking became universal? Would there be privacy or competitive risks?

4. How could your own business or career benefit from supply chains that are open, verifiable, and fraud-resistant?

Chapter 13

How Blockchain Is Revolutionizing Humanitarian Aid

Witness the role of blockchain in crisis zones, where it delivers aid faster, verifies every transaction, and ensures help reaches the people who need it most.

The Challenges of Humanitarian Aid

When disaster strikes, speed and transparency can mean the difference between life and death. Whether it is a hurricane devastating coastal towns, an earthquake leveling cities, or a conflict displacing millions, the world often responds with pledges of food, shelter, and medical support.

But the reality on the ground is rarely straightforward. Aid systems rely on intricate webs of government agencies, Global Non-Governmental Organizations, contractors, local suppliers, and financial intermediaries. Each adds paperwork, compliance checks, and manual reporting that slows down the process. In the chaos of emergencies, these layers become serious obstacles.

It is common for funds to sit idle in bureaucratic channels while people on the ground struggle to access clean water and medical supplies. Shipments of vital goods can be delayed by missing signatures or lost documentation. Local corruption sometimes diverts resources before they reach the intended recipients. This inefficiency is not just inconvenient; it can be devastating.

According to the United Nations Office for the Coordination of Humanitarian Affairs, roughly 35 percent of humanitarian aid funding never reaches its target, lost to overhead, duplication, or mismanagement. Trust is another casualty. Donors and taxpayers often wonder if their contributions actually help those in need.

The humanitarian sector is seeking better ways to ensure money and resources flow quickly, reach the right people, and leave an auditable trail that builds confidence. Blockchain technology is emerging as a transformative tool to solve exactly these problems.

A New Model of Trust and Efficiency
Blockchain introduces a radically different approach to managing aid distribution. Instead of relying on complex chains of paper records and siloed databases across dozens of agencies, blockchain creates a shared, tamper-resistant ledger. Each party can add information and verify the flow of funds or goods in real time.

This simple shift changes everything. Money and supplies can be tracked from the moment a pledge is made to when trucks deliver food to local warehouses, medical kits reach community clinics, and families redeem digital aid credits at neighborhood markets.

Since records on blockchain are immutable, it becomes nearly impossible to falsify delivery data or reroute assets without detection. Donors can see precisely how their contributions move through the system.

For local organizations, this means fewer delays. Smart contracts on blockchain can automate release of funds once specific conditions are met. For instance, when a verified shipment of medical equipment arrives at a designated clinic, payment can be triggered automatically. This eliminates waiting for manual approval and builds trust between international agencies and on-the-ground partners.

Real-World Stories of Blockchain in Action

Refugee Aid and Identity Protection

One of the most widely recognized examples of blockchain's humanitarian impact comes from the World Food Programme's Building Blocks initiative. In Jordan's Azraq and Zaatari refugee camps, home to over 100,000 Syrian refugees, the WFP uses blockchain to manage food and cash assistance.

Instead of relying on paper vouchers or third-party financial institutions, each refugee is registered on a secure blockchain platform tied to biometric data like an iris scan. When a mother walks into a supermarket in the camp, she looks into a scanner at checkout. Her identity is verified instantly against the blockchain ledger, and the payment is deducted from her aid balance.

There is no need for bank accounts or physical cash, reducing theft and financial exploitation. This system has processed hundreds of millions of dollars in aid, dramatically cutting transaction fees and administrative overhead. It also provides an immutable audit trail, so donors can verify that resources reach the intended recipients.

Stellar and Circle: Delivering Direct Payments

Blockchain's ability to support direct, cross-border cash transfers is gaining even more traction through partnerships with financial technology giants. Stellar's network, together with Circle's USDC stablecoin, is being used by organizations like the International Rescue Committee and Mercy Corps to deliver aid instantly across borders. Families in crisis zones can receive digital dollars directly on their phones, redeemable at local shops or through partners like MoneyGram, without waiting days for international bank wires or risking cash handlers. This approach slashes transfer costs, speeds up delivery, and gives vulnerable communities safer, faster access to emergency resources.

Restoring Trust After Disasters

Following major disasters, blockchain is also proving its worth in rebuilding efforts. After the earthquake in Haiti in 2010, billions were pledged, yet many projects stalled, and substantial portions of funds seemed to vanish in a haze of mismanagement. Similar frustrations emerged after Typhoon Haiyan struck the Philippines. Communities waited years for promised infrastructure and support.

By integrating blockchain into post-disaster funding models, organizations can enforce accountability at every step. Smart contracts tied to building milestones ensure that funds only release when work is independently verified. If a local contractor claims to have rebuilt 50 homes, payments trigger only when satellite imagery or third-party inspections confirm the progress. This structure not only deters fraud but accelerates recovery by cutting out repeated manual approvals.

Ethereum's Role in Transparent Humanitarian Cash
Many of these large-scale humanitarian systems run on private Ethereum-based ledgers. The World Food Programme's Building Blocks platform in Jordan uses Ethereum infrastructure to securely tie aid distributions to biometric scans, preventing fraud and reducing the overhead that traditionally eats into relief budgets. By using Ethereum's secure smart contract capabilities, the WFP has delivered substantial aid with unmatched transparency, building confidence among donors and local partners alike.

Tracking Medical Supplies in Crisis Zones

Maintaining trust is critical when it comes to health interventions. During the Ebola outbreak in West Africa, international agencies faced severe challenges tracking shipments of protective equipment and vaccines. Without unified, tamper-proof records, shipments could be misrouted, delayed, or even stolen.

Companies like Everledger, initially known for tracing diamonds, have applied blockchain to humanitarian medical supply chains. By logging every box of medical kits, every cold storage checkpoint, and every final delivery on blockchain, agencies can ensure critical resources reach hospitals and clinics without interference. Local staff scan QR codes to confirm receipt, instantly updating the global ledger.

This level of transparency means fewer stockouts, faster responses when inventory runs low, and concrete evidence that life-saving tools reach the communities they were intended for.

Empowering People with Direct Aid

Blockchain is not only helping track aid logistics. It is changing how help reaches individuals directly. In many developing regions, people impacted by disasters or conflict lack access to traditional bank accounts. This forces aid agencies to rely on local cash handlers, vouchers, or even physical drops of money, all of which invite leakage or theft.

Programs like Oxfam's UnBlocked Cash pilot in Vanuatu have demonstrated how blockchain changes this. Families received NFC cards tied to blockchain wallets. When they purchased food or household goods from local merchants, payments were executed on a blockchain platform. This provided instant settlement, full visibility for donors, and dignified choice for families, who could decide what their household needed most.

Vendors also benefited. They received payments immediately without waiting days or weeks for aid agencies to process invoices. The ledger ensured that every transaction was recorded, protecting merchants from disputes or delayed reimbursements.

Algorand for Climate and Development Resilience
Beyond emergency relief, Algorand's energy-efficient blockchain is increasingly chosen for environmental resilience projects. The United Nations Development Programme has piloted Algorand-based systems to certify carbon offset initiatives and climate adaptation work. By recording tree planting and clean energy installations on blockchain, local cooperatives can prove their impact transparently, unlocking

funding while preventing exaggerated claims that might siphon resources from truly at-risk communities.

Combating Corruption in Humanitarian Finance

Traditional aid flows through multiple hands: large international agencies, regional offices, local partners, and finally community groups. Each step adds paperwork and creates opportunities for funds to go missing. In some countries, corrupt officials have demanded bribes or siphoned funds meant for desperate families.

Blockchain rewrites this dynamic. Since transactions are logged on an open, tamper-resistant ledger, it becomes far harder for anyone to alter records or hide illicit transfers. Smart contracts can enforce pre-agreed spending rules. If a local health department receives funding to vaccinate 10,000 children, money can be disbursed in stages, tied to independently verified vaccination data.

This does not just protect resources. It rebuilds trust in the humanitarian system itself. Donors see exactly where their money goes. Governments under pressure to show accountability can point to blockchain records as proof of clean stewardship.

Supporting Small, Local Organizations

One of the most exciting aspects of blockchain in

humanitarian aid is how it levels the playing field for local nonprofits. Many small organizations do incredible work in their communities but lack the extensive paperwork systems demanded by major donors.

By using blockchain to record expenditures, deliveries, and outcomes, local NGOs can create real-time audit trails without hiring large compliance departments. This increases their credibility and opens doors to international funding.

Imagine a small women's cooperative running nutritional programs in rural Kenya. With a simple mobile interface, they record every kilogram of food purchased and every household served onto a blockchain. A European foundation funding the initiative can log in and see results instantly, without waiting months for printed reports.

Key Takeaways

• Blockchain creates tamper-resistant records that ensure funds, food, and medical supplies reach people faster and with full accountability

• It cuts down on corruption and misuse by logging every transaction transparently, protecting both donors and communities

• Programs by the World Food Programme, Oxfam, Stellar, Circle, Ethereum, and Algorand show how blockchain is transforming refugee support, direct cash aid, climate resilience, and health logistics

• Local organizations use blockchain to build trust with funders, proving impact without expensive administrative systems

---

Reflection Questions

1. How might knowing exactly where your donations go change how much or where you choose to give?

2. What risks or challenges do you see in shifting humanitarian aid to blockchain systems, especially in areas with weak digital infrastructure?

3. Could blockchain-powered transparency make governments more willing to fund large-scale relief efforts, knowing corruption risks are reduced?

4. How might local organizations in your community or country benefit from these tools to secure more resources and serve people better?

Chapter 14

Rebuilding Real Estate: Blockchain, Tokenization, and Ownership Reinvented

Discover how blockchain is being used to record ownership, eliminate fraud, enable fractional ownership, and turn NFTs into legal titles.

Real estate has always represented stability. Land, property, and buildings are some of the oldest, most recognized stores of wealth. But the process of buying, selling, and managing real estate has often been anything but stable. It is known for being slow, expensive, paperwork-heavy, and vulnerable to fraud. Blockchain is now transforming the foundations of this trillion-dollar industry.

At the core of that transformation are three elements: transparency, tokenization, and access. Together, they are reinventing how real estate is owned, financed, and transferred across the globe.

The Problem with Traditional Real Estate

Historically, real estate transactions have involved layers of intermediaries. Brokers, escrow agents, title companies, notaries, and banks all take part in a process that can stretch for weeks or months. Each step adds time, cost, and the potential for human error or fraud.

Even after a sale is completed, verifying ownership often requires physical deeds stored in government buildings or legal offices. Cross-border transactions introduce further complications with different legal systems, currencies, and regulations.

Blockchain removes the need to rely on trust in centralized systems. It replaces paper-based transactions with digital records that are immutable, verifiable, and globally accessible.

Blockchain as a Title System

One of the most immediate applications of blockchain in real estate is using it to record ownership. A blockchain-based title system can store the entire chain of custody of a property: who owned it, when it changed hands, and under what conditions. Because blockchain records are tamper-proof, ownership cannot be faked or altered retroactively.

In countries where land registries are unreliable or corrupt, this becomes especially powerful. In Georgia, the government partnered with Bitfury to use blockchain to register land titles. Since 2017, over 1.5 million land titles have been recorded on the blockchain, reducing fraud and increasing trust in the system.

Sweden has also explored blockchain-based land registries through Lantmäteriet, the national land survey. By digitizing the entire property transfer process, they found they could cut transaction times by up to 90 percent.

This level of efficiency and security creates a global precedent: blockchain can serve as the foundation for modern property records.

The Rise of Tokenized Real Estate

Tokenization is the process of converting real-world assets into digital tokens that can be traded on a blockchain. In the case of real estate, this means creating fractional shares of a property that can be bought and sold like digital assets.

Instead of needing hundreds of thousands or millions of dollars to purchase a property, an investor could buy a small fraction, even just a few dollars' worth, of a tokenized building. This democratizes access to real estate investing and unlocks liquidity in what has traditionally been an illiquid market.

Platforms like RealT in the United States are already making this possible. Properties are legally owned by LLCs, and ownership of the LLC is represented by tokens on the blockchain. Investors receive a portion of rental income directly to their wallets, often daily, in stablecoins like USDC.

Another example is Brickken, which enables asset owners to tokenize and sell portions of real estate on a decentralized marketplace. In doing so, they bypass traditional gatekeepers and reduce issuance costs.

Coldwell Banker, a global leader in real estate, has begun exploring blockchain-based property listings and digital ownership records, bringing mainstream recognition to tokenization.

What to Watch Out for in Tokenized Real Estate

As tokenized real estate gains momentum, it also faces growing challenges. In 2024 and 2025, several cases emerged where platforms were found to be tokenizing properties they did not fully control. Some platforms created tokens tied to properties still under legal dispute or falsely claimed ownership of assets never properly transferred into the entity managing the tokenization.

These incidents revealed an important truth: blockchain can verify who owns a token, but it cannot independently verify ownership of the physical asset behind it. That still depends on clear legal documentation, title verification, and trustworthy oversight.

To protect the integrity of tokenized real estate, new standards are being developed around compliance, custody, and verification. Still, participants must do their due diligence.

> Before engaging with a tokenized property, investors should always verify:
> • Who legally owns the property
> • What legal entity is tied to the token
> • Whether the offering complies with local laws and financial regulations

- If an independent custodian, legal trustee, or auditor oversees the asset

As the space evolves, reputable platforms are embracing greater transparency and integrating legal frameworks that align with real-world property laws. These measures will be critical for building long-term trust in tokenized real estate markets.

NFTs as Legal Titles

In addition to tokens that represent fractional shares, non-fungible tokens (NFTs) can serve as entire property titles. Each NFT is unique, making it ideal for representing a single, specific asset like a house or piece of land.

One high-profile example is Propy, a blockchain real estate platform that enables real estate purchases via smart contracts and NFTs. In 2021, they completed the first NFT-based real estate sale in the United States: a property in Florida sold entirely through an NFT title transfer. The process was fully transparent, legally compliant, and completed in minutes rather than weeks.

NFT titles can include more than just proof of ownership. They can store property history, inspection reports, liens, insurance, and even smart contract terms that automate future sales or rental agreements.

This fundamentally changes how ownership is managed. No more lost deeds, disputed transfers, or forged signatures. An NFT title lives on a secure, immutable ledger and can be accessed instantly.

Smart Contracts for Automated Transactions

Smart contracts are digital agreements that execute automatically when predefined conditions are met. In real estate, this opens the door to self-executing purchases, lease agreements, and escrow functions.

For instance, a smart contract can hold funds in escrow until a buyer receives verified property documents. Once the documents are confirmed, the contract releases the funds to the seller and transfers the ownership token to the buyer, all without third-party involvement.

Smart contracts also make rental agreements more efficient. A tenant can sign a lease and pay with cryptocurrency, and the smart contract automatically grants digital access and distributes payments to the landlord.

By automating these processes, smart contracts reduce the chance of disputes, delay, and miscommunication.

Global Access, Fractional Ownership, and New Markets

One of the most transformative aspects of blockchain real estate is global access. A property in Tokyo could be tokenized and purchased in part by investors in Brazil, Nigeria, or Canada. This opens real estate markets to international capital without the usual regulatory or currency barriers.

Fractional ownership also lowers the barrier for individuals to begin investing. A young professional might not be able to buy a condo, but they could invest fifty dollars into ten properties across different cities. This diversifies their portfolio and introduces wealth-building opportunities previously out of reach.

This also creates opportunities for developers and communities. A new housing development could crowdfund its construction through token sales, giving future residents or supporters a stake in the project from the beginning.

Challenges and Regulations

Despite the enormous potential, tokenized real estate still faces regulatory and legal hurdles. In many jurisdictions, property laws have not yet caught up with blockchain. There are questions about how tokens are classified, how taxes apply, and how to enforce rights across borders.

Projects like Propy, RealT, and Roofstock onChain are actively working with regulators to navigate these complexities. Over time, we can expect to see clearer frameworks that support the adoption of blockchain-based real estate systems.

The Future of Ownership

Blockchain is not simply digitizing real estate. It is reprogramming the very concept of ownership.

It enables secure, instant transfers of value. It creates global, round-the-clock marketplaces. It gives access to individuals who were previously locked out. And it builds transparency into a system that for too long relied on trust without verification.

Property is one of the most foundational aspects of wealth. With blockchain, it becomes more accessible, more transparent, and more aligned with the speed and structure of our digital world.

Key Takeaways

• Blockchain enables tamper-proof digital land titles, reducing fraud and delays in real estate transactions

• Tokenization allows fractional ownership of property, lowering the barrier to entry for investors

• NFTs can represent entire property titles and include legal documentation, ownership history, and smart contract terms

• Smart contracts automate property sales, lease agreements, and escrow functions

• Global investors can now access property markets previously limited by geography or regulation

---

Reflection Questions

1. What aspects of traditional real estate have you experienced as slow, expensive, or inaccessible?

2. How might fractional ownership change your perspective on investing in property?

3. What new opportunities might blockchain-based real estate open up in your community or region?

4. Could NFTs replace traditional property titles in the future? What would need to change in your local area for that to happen?

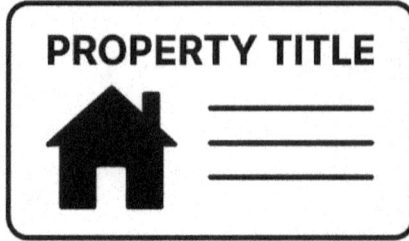

REBUILDING
REAL ESTATE

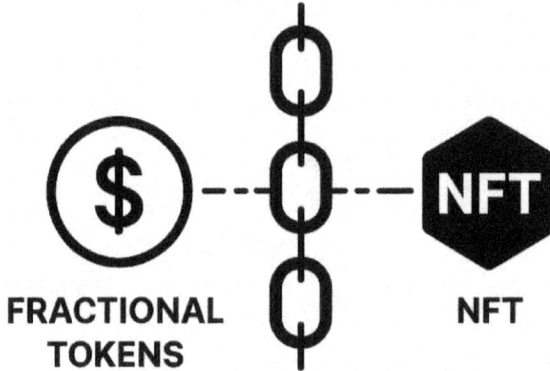

FRACTIONAL TOKENS

NFT

- RECORD OWNERSHIP
- ELIMINATE FRAUD
- FRACTIONAL OWNERSHIP

Chapter 15

How Blockchain Is Transforming Finance and Lending

Traditional financial systems are being disrupted by blockchain, opening access to new forms of capital, credit, and peer-to-peer lending.

For decades, the traditional financial system has depended on layers of intermediaries, delayed settlements, and institutional gatekeeping. Access to capital has been limited by geography, credit scores, and outdated banking processes. But blockchain is changing that, not by improving the current system, but by replacing its foundation.

We're entering an era where financial services run on code instead of paperwork. Where access is global, immediate, and programmable. Where anyone with a smartphone and a wallet can earn yield, take out a loan, or participate in capital markets without ever stepping into a bank.

This shift isn't on the horizon. It's happening now.

From Centralized Banking to Programmable Money

In the legacy system, money sits in checking accounts that pay nothing. Savings accounts barely outpace inflation. Investments require approvals and minimum balances. And borrowing is often slow, expensive, and wrapped in red tape.

Blockchain reverses that.

With smart contracts and self-executing code on the blockchain, money becomes programmable. You can tell it where to go, what to do, and under what conditions. That's not just innovation. That's a complete rewiring of financial logic.

The Programmable Paycheck: Real-Time Finance

Imagine getting paid on a Friday and watching your income instantly divide across a personalized financial ecosystem with no middlemen, no delays, and no friction. Here's what that could look like:

- 45% into a high yield stablecoin vault earning 5% or more through decentralized lending protocols
- 25% into a staking pool supporting major networks and generating daily rewards
- 20% into a liquidity pool earning yield as users trade between popular token pairs
- 10% into tokenized real-world assets with ongoing revenue distribution

Every dollar is optimized the moment it arrives. Yield begins the second your paycheck hits your wallet. And you retain full control over every transaction, no permissions, no bank approvals, no delays.

These smart contract systems already exist across blockchains like Ethereum, Stellar, and Solana. Projects like Aave, Compound, and Yield Protocol make it possible to automate your financial flow and generate returns immediately, not in weeks, months, or years.

Instant Lending Without Banks

Traditional lending is built around paperwork, FICO scores, and manual underwriting. It's slow. It's exclusive. And it's expensive.

DeFi lending flips the model. Instead of asking "Are you approved?" the question becomes "Do you have collateral?"

If you do, you can borrow instantly. Here's how it works:

1. You deposit an asset like ETH, XRP, or USDC into a smart contract.

2. You receive a percentage of that value as a loan in another token, sometimes in seconds.

3. Your collateral stays locked until you repay, or the value drops below a certain threshold.

No credit check. No waiting. And no need to trust a centralized institution. The code handles everything.

This system is already powering billions in loans across platforms like MakerDAO, Venus, and JustLend. And it's expanding fast, not just for tech-savvy users, but for emerging economies where traditional lending is inaccessible.

Peer-to-Peer Lending at Scale

Blockchain also enables true peer-to-peer lending, where people lend directly to others with smart contracts enforcing terms.

Platforms like Goldfinch and Maple Finance let institutional or individual investors fund loans to real-world businesses in places where capital is scarce. Returns are paid directly to lenders through the blockchain, with full transparency.

Unlike traditional microloans, which rely on intermediaries and overhead, blockchain lending operates with minimal friction. Risk is managed through collateral, staking, insurance pools, and borrower reputation systems.

This opens the door to a more connected financial ecosystem, where opportunity flows freely across borders and communities.

Yield-Bearing Wallets and Always-On Earnings

In the blockchain economy, idle money is wasted money. Tokens can be deposited into:

- **Liquidity pools** on decentralized exchanges like Uniswap or Stellar AMMs, earning fees on every trade

- **Staking contracts** where users secure a network and earn native token rewards

- **Lending protocols** that pay interest for supplying liquidity

Even stablecoins, digital dollars like USDC, RLUSD, or EURC, can generate 4 to 7 percent yield in well-established protocols with minimal volatility.

This means that the portion of your money sitting "in cash" doesn't have to sit idle. It can grow. And you can still access it whenever needed.

In this model, every financial tool works harder. Every token has a job. And the boundaries between savings, investment, and liquidity begin to dissolve.

Institutional Momentum Is Building

Major financial institutions aren't ignoring this. They're building on top of it.

- **JPMorgan** has launched blockchain-based collateral settlements and tokenized money market funds

- **Visa** and **Mastercard** are exploring stablecoin-based settlements for global payments

- **BlackRock** and **Franklin Templeton** are tokenizing funds and offering blockchain-native investment vehicles

- **Coinbase** now allows users to earn 5%+ on RLUSD directly within the app, a sign of how mainstream this model is becoming

As these systems mature, they won't just coexist with traditional finance. They'll transform it from the inside out.

The Road Ahead: Finance Without Friction

The future of finance is automated, optimized, and on-chain. It's a world where:

- Paychecks earn yield before you spend them

- Borrowing is instant, fair, and global

- Financial tools are open-source and composable

- Value moves in seconds, not days

This puts individuals at the center of the financial system.

Blockchain doesn't replace money. It reprograms it for a new era.

And that era is already here.

Key Takeaways

• Blockchain enables programmable money, allowing income and spending to be automated through smart contracts

• DeFi platforms allow users to earn yield, take loans, and invest without banks or credit checks

• Stablecoins like USDC and RLUSD can generate real yield while remaining liquid and accessible

• Institutions are adopting blockchain for payments, lending, and asset management

• The future of finance is real-time, global, and user-controlled

---

Reflection Questions

1. How would your financial life change if your income was automatically optimized the moment you earned it?

2. What traditional financial tools could be replaced by smart contracts in your current routine?

3. What role do you want to play in shaping the next evolution of finance, user, builder, or investor?

Chapter 16

The Future of Contracts: Smart Contracts and Automated Agreements

Contracts are no longer just paperwork. They are becoming programmable, self-executing, and more secure than ever before.

Contracts have always been at the heart of how people and organizations do business. They define expectations, set obligations, and establish trust. Yet for centuries, they have been static, paper-based, and dependent on lawyers, intermediaries, and often slow-moving processes. That is changing. Blockchain has given rise to a new generation of agreements that are programmable, self-executing, and far more secure than traditional contracts. These are called smart contracts, and they are not only transforming the speed and cost of doing business, they are reshaping what a contract can be.

What Is a Smart Contract?

A smart contract is a digital agreement stored on a blockchain that automatically executes when predefined conditions are met. Unlike traditional contracts, there is no need for manual enforcement or oversight. The terms are embedded in the code, and once they are in place, the contract runs exactly as programmed. This eliminates ambiguity, reduces the risk of fraud, and cuts out many of the delays associated with human processing.

Smart contracts were first conceptualized in the 1990s by cryptographer Nick Szabo, but they became practical and widely used with the launch of blockchain platforms like

Ethereum in 2015. Today, they are being adopted across industries, from finance and real estate to supply chains and entertainment.

How Smart Contracts Work

Smart contracts operate through a straightforward process:

1. **Agreement is Defined** — The parties agree on the terms, which are then translated into code.

2. **Conditions are Programmed** — Specific triggers or events are defined, such as a date, payment amount, or delivery confirmation.

3. **Execution is Automated** — When the conditions are met, the contract executes automatically.

4. **Results are Recorded** — The blockchain records the transaction, creating a permanent, tamper-proof record.

Because the process is automated and transparent, it removes the need for trust between the parties. The contract's integrity comes from the blockchain itself.

Atomic Settlement: Simultaneous and Secure Exchanges

Atomic settlement is a process in which all parts of a transaction such as delivering an asset, updating ownership records, and transferring payment are completed instantly and as one indivisible action. In other words, either every step happens successfully, or nothing happens at all.

This approach eliminates counterparty risk, the possibility that one party fulfills their obligation while the other fails to do so. Because the exchange is programmed to be conditional and simultaneous, there is no moment where one side is left exposed. For example, if a digital asset is being sold for tokenized currency, the smart contract ensures that the seller only releases the asset at the exact same moment the buyer's payment is received on-chain.

The benefits extend far beyond security:

- **Shorter Settlement Times** — Traditional cross-border settlements can take days or even weeks due to banking cut-off times, intermediary verification, and manual reconciliation. Atomic settlement reduces this to seconds or minutes, regardless of time zones.

- **Lower Costs** — By removing the need for multiple intermediaries, custodians, or clearinghouses, the transaction process becomes leaner and less expensive.

- **Increased Transparency** — Every action is recorded on the blockchain in real time, creating a permanent, tamper-proof audit trail that regulators, auditors, or counterparties can verify instantly.

- **Greater Liquidity** — With faster settlement, capital is freed up sooner, allowing both individuals and institutions to redeploy funds into new opportunities without waiting for traditional settlement cycles to complete.

In decentralized finance (DeFi), atomic swaps allow cryptocurrency traders to exchange assets across different blockchains without the need for a centralized exchange. In regulated finance, projects like Canada's Project Jasper and Singapore's Project Ubin have proven that atomic settlement can be applied to central bank digital currencies (CBDCs), paving the way for near-instant, risk-free settlement in global markets.

The result is a transaction model that not only accelerates the pace of business but also fundamentally changes the trust structure of financial systems, shifting reliance from human oversight to cryptographic certainty.

Examples of Real-World Atomic Settlement Implementations

1. Goldman Sachs – Atomic Settlement with Tokenized Bonds

In 2022, Goldman Sachs issued a €100 million two-year digital bond for the European Investment Bank using its Digital Asset Platform (GS DAP). The bond issuance, settlement, and record-keeping all took place on-chain with instant "atomic" delivery-vs-payment execution—meaning the bond and payment were exchanged simultaneously, in under 60 seconds. This was a breakthrough demonstration of atomic settlement being used in a regulated, institutional context.

2. mBridge – Multi-CBDC Cross-Border Atomic Settlement

Led by the Bank for International Settlements Innovation Hub in partnership with the central banks of China, Hong Kong, Thailand, and the United Arab Emirates, **mBridge** is a working platform for fast, secure cross-border payments using wholesale central bank digital currencies. It supports atomic settlement, ensuring funds and payment messages are processed simultaneously across different jurisdictions, eliminating delays and settlement risk.

Real-World Examples of Smart Contracts

Major organizations are integrating them into their operations today.

- **Finance and Banking** — JPMorgan Chase has developed blockchain-based platforms like Onyx that use smart contracts to streamline payment settlements between institutions in minutes instead of days.

- **Supply Chains** — IBM's Food Trust platform uses smart contracts to track food from farm to table, ensuring safety and authenticity at every step.

- **Insurance** — Companies like AXA have experimented with flight delay insurance that automatically pays travelers if their flight is late, without requiring a claim form.

- **Entertainment** — Musicians are using smart contracts to receive instant royalties every time their song is streamed, with platforms like Opulous and Royal leading the way.

- **Real Estate** — Propy has facilitated blockchain-based real estate transactions where smart contracts handle escrow, title transfer, and payment in one secure, automated process.

Dubai's Leading Smart Contract Examples

Dubai has positioned itself as a global leader in applying blockchain-powered agreements to real-world sectors, especially in real estate.

A. Dubai Land Department (DLD) — Real Estate Tokenization

- The DLD's Real Estate Tokenization Project under the "REES" framework is the first government-led tokenization program in the Middle East.

- Enables fractional property ownership through blockchain-based tokens.

- Allows investment starting at AED 2,000 (~USD 545).

- Targets tokenizing AED 60 billion (~USD 16 billion) in real estate by 2033.

- Smart contracts handle payment-triggered ownership transfers and instant registry updates.

B. Smart Contracts for Property Transactions and Transparency

- The DLD was the first government body globally to integrate blockchain-based contracting for real estate.

- Links property records, utility registrations, and identity verification systems directly to the blockchain.

- Over 40% of transactions now use smart contracts, delivering:

  - Transfers in under 72 hours.

  - Fraud reduction of 67%.

  - Administrative cost savings of 30%.

Why Smart Contracts Matter

Smart contracts bring a level of speed, precision, and security that traditional contracts cannot match. They reduce reliance on third parties, cut transaction times from days to seconds, and lower costs by removing intermediaries. They also ensure that terms are enforced exactly as agreed, which reduces disputes and legal expenses.

Beyond efficiency, smart contracts create entirely new possibilities. They can be programmed to interact with other contracts, form decentralized applications or even govern autonomous organizations without human intervention.

Challenges and Limitations

While the benefits are clear, there are still hurdles to overcome:

- **Coding Accuracy** — A smart contract will execute exactly as written, so errors in code can create costly mistakes.

- **Legal Recognition** — Some jurisdictions have not yet updated their laws to fully recognize blockchain-based contracts.

- **Scalability** — High transaction volumes can cause delays or higher fees on some blockchains.

- **Security Risks** — If a contract is hacked, funds or assets can be stolen instantly.

As the technology matures, these challenges are being addressed through better development tools, updated regulations, and hybrid approaches that combine smart contracts with traditional oversight.

The Role of Smart Contracts in Emerging Economies

In regions where legal systems are slow or unreliable, smart contracts can be transformative. They provide a neutral, tamper-proof way to enforce agreements without the need for expensive legal intervention. This is particularly powerful in global trade, where buyers and sellers often operate across borders and legal systems.

For example, small business owners in developing countries can now sell goods internationally with smart contracts guaranteeing payment upon delivery. This opens up new markets and increases economic opportunity without the traditional barriers of cross-border transactions.

Integrating Smart Contracts into the Metaverse and Web3

Smart contracts are also the foundation of the metaverse and decentralized applications in Web3. They govern virtual land sales, in-game economies, and NFT transactions. In these environments, ownership and access rights are determined entirely by blockchain logic, ensuring that transactions are secure and enforceable without a central authority.

Platforms like Decentraland and The Sandbox rely on smart contracts to manage every transfer of virtual assets. This creates a seamless bridge between digital ownership and real-world value.

The Next Evolution — Automated Agreements

The next step for smart contracts is deeper integration with artificial intelligence and real-world data through oracles. Oracles feed external information, such as market prices or weather reports, into a blockchain so that smart contracts can respond to real-world events.

For example:

- Agricultural insurance contracts can automatically pay farmers if satellite data shows drought conditions.

- Freight contracts can release payment when GPS data confirms that goods have arrived at the correct location.

- Energy contracts can adjust pricing in real time based on consumption data.

This combination of blockchain, AI, and real-time data is making contracts not just digital, but intelligent.

Key Takeaways

• Smart contracts are self-executing agreements stored on a blockchain that run automatically when predefined conditions are met.

• They reduce the need for intermediaries, speed up transactions, and provide transparency and security.

• Atomic settlement enables simultaneous, risk-free exchange of assets and payments, with global pilot projects paving the way for broader adoption.

• Dubai is leading government-level adoption of smart contracts, especially in real estate tokenization and automated property transfers.

• While challenges remain, the potential to transform how we create, enforce, and interact with contracts is immense.

Reflection Questions

1. How could your organization use smart contracts to reduce costs, increase trust, or speed up transactions?

2. What legal or operational barriers might you face in adopting blockchain-based agreements?

3. How could AI and real-time data integration improve the functionality of contracts in your industry?

4. Are there areas of your business that would benefit from automated execution rather than manual oversight?

5. How could smart contracts help you engage with global markets and partners more effectively?

SMART CONTRACTS & AUTOMATED AGREEMENTS

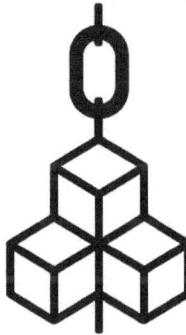

- EXECUTION BY CODE
- TRUSTLESS TRANSACTIONS

Chapter 17

Redefining Growth Through Blockchain and Belonging

Blockchain is reshaping personal growth, community, and creative ecosystems by linking human potential with digital innovation, creating new models of participation, ownership, and value.

Every era of change has its defining movements, not just technologies that improve efficiency, but frameworks that reimagine how people live, connect, and grow. The internet gave us new ways to communicate. Smartphones placed the world in our hands. Now blockchain is building the foundation for ecosystems where value, identity, and creativity flow directly between people and communities.

Center for Creators stands as one of these movements. It merges blockchain infrastructure with personal growth and digital ownership in ways designed to expand human potential. This is where personal development meets programmable assets, where creative work can be minted, shared, and rewarded on-chain, and where belonging itself becomes part of an economy that recognizes and amplifies contribution.

Around the world, education systems, cultural initiatives, and community-driven platforms are beginning to explore similar possibilities. From blockchain diplomas at MIT to global learning records through the Learning Economy Foundation, and digital identity projects at Arizona State University with Sony, the momentum is clear. Yet Center for Creators brings a distinct focus: it shows how blockchain can serve not just institutions, but individuals, transforming growth itself into a digital asset that can be proven, exchanged, and expanded.

Building an Ecosystem for Human Potential

Center for Creators began as a vision to merge personal development with cutting-edge blockchain systems. The CFC Token, launched in 2021 on the XRP Ledger, quickly gained traction, ranking in the top 1 percent of over 9,300 tokens within its first two weeks. The rapid response revealed something important. People were ready for a model that connected personal transformation to the mechanics of the digital economy.

At its core, the platform provides an ecosystem where growth, contribution, and creativity are not abstract ideas but measurable, verifiable, and exchangeable. Members can access workshops, coaching, events, and programs where each experience is tokenized as a non-fungible token (NFT). These NFTs are secured with smart contracts, which automatically handle ownership, access rights, and even revenue sharing. The result is a system where trust does not need to be outsourced, because blockchain provides the proof.

Personal Growth Meets Tokenization

In traditional systems, personal development is difficult to measure or preserve. A completed course, a leadership retreat, or even a transformative mentorship often leaves no lasting credential that others can easily recognize or verify. Center for Creators changes this by allowing workshops, coaching sessions, and learning experiences to be minted as NFTs. Each NFT contains proof of participation, authenticity, and outcomes that can be shared across industries, communities, or future opportunities.

For example, a participant who completes a leadership workshop can receive a blockchain-verified NFT credential. This credential cannot be forged or lost and can be used to demonstrate growth in professional or academic settings. At the same time, creators who deliver these workshops or events gain a direct and transparent revenue channel, with payments distributed instantly through smart contracts. No delays, no intermediaries, and no uncertainty.

Expanding Creative Economies

The platform also functions as a launchpad for creators across disciplines. Artists, writers, educators, and coaches can package their services or works as tokenized offerings, directly accessible to their audience. A book can be minted as an NFT with accompanying exclusive content. A wellness retreat can be token-gated so only verified participants gain access. A coaching program can use smart contracts to distribute revenue automatically between facilitators and collaborators.

This structure builds a community-driven economy where contribution is rewarded and loyalty is recognized. Participants are no longer just consumers. They become stakeholders in an ecosystem where their engagement has measurable value.

Specialized Communities: The Pickleball Coin

Beyond personal growth and professional development, Center for Creators extends into lifestyle communities. One example is Pickleball Coin (PBC), a utility token designed for the sport of pickleball. Players earn tokens by participating in verified matches and activities. These tokens can be exchanged for training sessions, equipment, event entry, or facility improvements.

The model shows how blockchain can connect recreation with infrastructure development. A local club that needs new courts can use Pickleball Coin to fund construction while engaging its community in the process. Every game becomes not only play but also contribution to something larger. Participation transforms into collective impact.

Education as a Parallel Evolution

While Center for Creators highlights the potential of merging growth with tokenized ecosystems, the education sector provides further evidence of how blockchain can reshape human development on a systemic level.

At the Massachusetts Institute of Technology (MIT), graduates have received blockchain-based diplomas that allow them to instantly verify their credentials with employers. This system bypasses the delays and costs of transcript requests while reducing fraud. The Learning Economy Foundation has introduced global learning records designed to track educational progress from childhood to professional life. Students and workers retain lifelong credentials that move with them, portable and provable anywhere in the world.

Arizona State University has partnered with Sony to explore digital identity solutions that protect student information while enabling seamless verification. Together, these efforts demonstrate how blockchain is not only making education more transparent but also more personal and enduring.

By placing Center for Creators alongside these examples, it becomes clear that the convergence of personal growth, creative economies, and education is an emerging reality where blockchain secures both knowledge and contribution.

Smart Contracts and Trust in Action

Central to this model is the role of smart contracts. These programmable agreements ensure that transactions occur only when conditions are met. In Center for Creators, a smart contract can release payment when a service is completed, issue a credential upon workshop participation, or grant access to an event once a token is verified.

The benefits extend to fairness, transparency, and efficiency. Service providers receive payment without delays. Participants know that their credentials are authentic. Communities see that value is distributed according to the rules encoded on-chain. Trust is no longer negotiated. It is embedded into the infrastructure itself.

Moving into the Metaverse and Beyond

Looking forward, Center for Creators is developing immersive environments in the metaverse. These spaces are designed for workshops, performances, masterminds, and global collaboration. Here, token ownership governs access, ensuring that participants gain value proportionate to their contribution and commitment.

At the same time, conscious artificial intelligence is being integrated into the ecosystem to personalize growth paths. AI can recommend resources, design learning plans, and even facilitate collaboration between creators and audiences. The goal is not only to expand reach but also to align growth with values, ethics, and well-being.

Blockchain-Based Publishing

Publishing is another area where Center for Creators pushes boundaries. Books, articles, and creative works can be minted as NFTs, giving readers ownership of verifiable copies while unlocking exclusive content. Authors retain full rights and gain direct relationships with their audiences. This model extends to academic publishing, where collaborative research can be verified, distributed, and cited on-chain.

The CFC Rewards DApp and Utility in Action

This same vision carries into the CFC Rewards DApp, which extends the principles of blockchain publishing into everyday engagement. For readers of *The Power to Rise*, activities inspired by the book become more than reflections on a page. They translate into blockchain-verified actions, where completing exercises, engaging with principles, or joining discussions generates CFC Tokens that can be redeemed for programs, workshops, or immersive events.

The Rewards DApp also extends beyond individual readers. Organizations can establish tokenized communities where employees earn tokens for wellness initiatives, innovation challenges, or professional development. Residential and commercial tenants can be rewarded for sustainability practices, feedback, or participation in local events. Each community defines its own rules and redemption pathways, yet all operate on the same underlying framework.

This is what makes the CFC Token a true utility token. Its value comes from the ability to claim and redeem it for real services, programs, workshops, or events across multiple ecosystems. Whether in publishing, education, workplace culture, or housing, the token provides direct access and tangible benefits. Every action that contributes to growth or community well-being can be exchanged for something meaningful, creating a transparent and provable loop of engagement.

The result is an economy of belonging where personal growth and collective contribution are inseparable. Progress is no longer abstract. It is visible, measurable, and redeemable, reinforcing both individual purpose and the strength of the communities we build together.

Key Takeaways

• Center for Creators demonstrates how blockchain can merge personal development, creative ownership, and tokenized community into one integrated ecosystem
• Smart contracts and NFTs ensure transparency, fairness, and efficiency across workshops, services, events, and publishing
• Education examples from MIT, the Learning Economy Foundation, and Arizona State University with Sony show how blockchain is transforming lifelong learning and credentialing
• Pickleball Coin highlights how lifestyle and recreation can be connected to community infrastructure through tokenized participation
• By uniting growth, creativity, and belonging, Center for Creators illustrates a model where human potential itself becomes part of the blockchain economy

---

Reflection Questions

1. How might ecosystems like Center for Creators reshape the way individuals build personal and professional value over a lifetime?

2. What opportunities exist for your community or industry to tokenize services, participation, or growth experiences?

3. How can blockchain credentialing, as seen at MIT and with the Learning Economy Foundation, inspire new ways of tracking and rewarding progress?

4. In what ways could tokenized recreation, such as Pickleball Coin, apply to other sports or activities to build stronger communities?

5. What possibilities emerge when creative ownership, personal growth, and education are all secured and expanded through blockchain?

Chapter 18

There's No Switch That's Going to Be Flipped

How the Shift to Blockchain Is a Global Process Unfolding
System by System.

Change at the scale of a new foundational technology never arrives with a single moment when everyone moves at once. The internet did not become essential because someone turned it on in a single day. The same is true for blockchain. Adoption happens in layers, within existing organizations, inside regulations that already exist, and through people who still need to run daily operations. In this chapter we look closely at how that quiet shift is unfolding system by system, where it is already visible, and how the next steps will build on what is working today.

From Big Idea to Quiet Infrastructure

Every transformative technology begins with a period of experimentation and debate. Then something more practical happens. Teams find specific use cases where the new approach solves a clear problem faster, cheaper, or with better reliability. In blockchain, that move from exploration to utility is visible in payments, asset issuance, compliance, and provenance. None of these are splashy announcements. They are infrastructure upgrades that make existing processes more resilient.

Banks settle value with tokenized cash or stablecoins when that reduces reconciliation. Logistics firms record the movement of goods on shared ledgers when that reduces disputes. Media and gaming companies use smart contracts when that reduces administrative overhead. The pattern is consistent across sectors. Start with a narrow problem. Prove that a shared ledger with programmable rules reduces friction. Expand to adjacent processes once trust has been established.

Why There Is No Single Switch

Three realities shape this transition.

First, institutions must remain compliant while they modernize. That means new systems need to connect to existing controls, audit practices, and reporting. Blockchain solutions that can plug into those realities move first.

Second, consumers will not change behavior simply because a new technology exists. They adopt the experiences that feel familiar, safer, and faster. A wallet that feels like a banking app. A checkout that looks like what they already use. A receipt that satisfies their accountant.

Third, global alignment takes time. A settlement flow that touches several countries must respect different legal codes, tax rules, and privacy requirements. Interoperability and standards therefore become the decisive enablers.

The Stack That Is Emerging

The shift is not only about ledgers. It is about a full stack that works end to end.

Identity and credentials give people and organizations portable proofs. Payment rails convert between bank money and digital tokens without adding new risk. Smart contracts automate business logic. Oracles and messaging frameworks move verified data into those contracts. Compliance services provide screening, reporting, and controls. Custody and key management protect access in ways that match institutional policy. Interoperability layers connect separate networks so value and information can move safely between them.

You can see this stack forming in live systems. Regulated institutions use permissioned chains for settlement while connecting to public networks for liquidity and distribution. Consumer experiences hide cryptography behind flows that feel normal. Developers build with software kits that abstract the complexity of nodes and signatures. The result is not a brand-new economy all at once. It is the existing economy with fewer delays, fewer errors, and fewer manual reconciliations.

Finance Is Converting Workflows One Link at a Time

Payments and settlement were early candidates for change because time and certainty matter. Stablecoin settlement for card programs, treasury movements, and cross border transfers is no longer unusual. Tokenized deposits are being piloted to let banks move value on programmable rails while holding to existing supervision. Market infrastructure operators are exploring digital issuance and atomic delivery versus payment so that assets and cash exchange at the exact same instant.

Asset management is following a similar pattern. Funds issued on chain can handle transfer restrictions and reporting through smart contracts. Transfer agents and administrators still perform their roles, yet with event streams that are transparent and easier to audit. Secondary trading of tokenized assets remains gated by regulation, but pilots continue to increase volumes. Over time, operational savings and faster distribution become compelling reasons to expand.

Supply Chains and Product Provenance Are Standardizing on Shared Truth

When the path from origin to destination spans continents, companies need a way to agree on events without relying on a single database. Shared ledgers give every participant the same view of milestones. Inputs are registered, transformations are recorded, and handoffs are notarized. The benefits start with fewer disputes and faster recalls. They grow into lower financing costs when lenders trust the data and are willing to advance capital against inventory or receivables with less risk.

Agriculture, food, pharmaceuticals, and luxury goods are seeing the most traction. The pattern is to begin with a single product line, demonstrate that counterfeit and waste drop, then invite suppliers and logistics partners to join. Once the data foundation exists, automation follows. Smart contracts can release payment at delivery confirmation, insurers can price risk from verified histories, and regulators can review records without waiting for monthly reports.

Real Estate and Physical Assets Are Becoming More Liquid

Property registries that move to tamper resistant databases reduce fraud and speed closings. When the registry is tied to a token that represents the legal interest, fractional investment becomes practical within a clear legal wrapper. Rental income and distributions can be paid programmatically. Secondary trading can be controlled so that eligibility and disclosures are enforced by code instead of by manual checks.

Markets that combine clear title, digital identity, and on chain issuance are starting to show lower friction for both local and foreign investors. This is not speculation about the future. It is a modernization of the same real estate processes that buyers and sellers already use, with fewer intermediaries and fewer chances for human error.

Public Sector Momentum

Governments are adopting blockchain where transparency and auditability serve the public. Land registries and permit systems become easier to verify. Procurement records and grant disbursements can be monitored in real time. Customs documentation and export controls benefit from a shared record of provenance and certifications. Central banks are running pilots for digital currency in both wholesale and retail contexts, with a focus on finality, privacy, and interoperability with existing payment systems.

The important pattern is measured rollout. Agencies pick high value processes with limited complexity. They run controlled pilots. They maintain compatibility with existing records. They teach staff and vendors. Then they scale.

Interoperability Is the Bridge Between Islands

No single chain will serve every need. Networks must exchange messages and assets safely. Interoperability frameworks are doing for blockchain what routing standards did for the early internet. They allow private networks, public chains, and legacy systems to speak in a common language.

This has two effects. First, it protects investment because a process that works on one network can talk to another without a full rebuild. Second, it reduces fragmentation. Liquidity and data do not have to live in silos. A lender can verify collateral on a supply chain network and settle a loan on a financial network. A regulator can observe activity across venues without demanding that everyone use the same technology stack.

Compliance, Privacy, and Risk Management Are Built In

Modern deployments embed controls rather than adding them later. Screening and monitoring tools plug into wallets, custodians, and transaction flows. Role based permissions determine who can view sensitive data. Zero knowledge techniques allow a party to prove compliance with a rule without revealing the underlying information. Event logs and analytics give auditors continuous assurance instead of periodic samples.

Institutions care deeply about operational risk. Key management, disaster recovery, and incident response are treated with the same rigor used for core banking systems. Service level expectations are defined. Vendors are reviewed and certified. The result is a path that lets blockchain based processes meet the same standards that existing systems meet today.

People and Process Matter as Much as Code

Technology does not change organizations on its own. Training, incentives, and change management are decisive. Teams that succeed explain the benefits in plain language. They measure time saved and errors avoided. They solve the help desk problems that keep deployments from scaling. They adjust job roles so that automation reduces repetition without creating confusion. They create internal centers of excellence so that lessons from one project accelerate the next.

What Leaders Are Doing Right Now

Leaders choose a narrow scope where they can win quickly. They pick a partner ecosystem that will stand up the required stack. They ensure legal and risk teams are involved from the start. They establish data standards with trading partners so that records can be verified across systems. They run a pilot with real users and real volume. They publish the outcome internally. Then they expand to the next process that benefits from the same foundation.

Consider several representative examples that illustrate this pattern.

A global payments network settles a portion of merchant payouts in a regulated stablecoin because it clears on weekends, gives instant visibility, and reduces the need for pre funding. A large asset manager issues a share class of a money market fund on a public network so transfer agents and distributors can reconcile positions without nightly batch files. A national land office links its registry to a blockchain based issuance system so lenders can verify title status in minutes rather than days. A mineral supply chain consortium ties certifications to shipments so exporters and importers can comply with regulations using verified records rather than email attachments.

Each example begins with something that already exists. Each adds shared truth and programmable logic. Each cuts out delays, errors, or disputes. None requires the entire economy to move at once.

How This Unfolds Over the Next Few Years

Several reinforcing waves are now in motion.

Payments and settlement continue to move toward instant finality with tokenized cash and atomic delivery versus payment. Asset issuance expands from single funds and bonds to broader catalogs as administrators and exchanges become comfortable with digital transfer restrictions and on chain reporting. Supply chain provenance becomes a requirement in more sectors as regulators and customers demand proof of origin and ethical sourcing. Identity and credentials move from pilots to production for education, professional licensing, and access management. Interoperability matures so that private networks connect to public liquidity and to legacy enterprise systems without custom bridges.

As these waves overlap, network effects grow. A company that starts with provenance gains the ability to finance inventory at better terms. An issuer that moves funds on chain discovers it can integrate with a marketplace for distribution. A government that digitizes land titles can enable fractional investment inside clear rules. Each success attracts more participants, which in turn raises the value of participating. This is how a quiet change becomes the default way of doing things.

Practical Guidance for Readers

You do not need to rebuild everything. Begin with an area where time, transparency, or trust are genuine bottlenecks. Map the current process and identify the manual handoffs that add delay or cost. Decide what must be private and what can be shared. Choose partners who can supply identity, custody, compliance, and interoperability out of the box. Run a production grade pilot with clear metrics. Share results with the people who will rely on the system. Expand in concentric circles.

Think of the adoption curve as a series of wins. If a new workflow reduces settlement from two days to two minutes, measure that. If on chain events reduce disputes by half, measure that. If auditors can complete a review in hours rather than weeks because the ledger is transparent, measure that. Those measurements become the business case for the next phase.

A New Kind of Default

At some point people stop talking about blockchain and start talking only about the experience. Funds arrive when expected even on weekends. Ownership records update in minutes. Compliance checks run in the background. Supply chain data is trusted without argument. Developers assemble applications from modules that already solve identity, payment, and policy. That is the meaning of no switch being flipped. The future arrives piece by piece until it becomes the default.

Key Takeaways

• Blockchain adoption grows through practical upgrades to existing systems rather than sudden replacement

• Interoperability, identity, compliance, and custody form the stack that makes adoption safe and repeatable

• Finance, supply chains, real estate, and public sector processes are converting to shared ledgers where they cut delays, errors, and disputes

• Atomic settlement and tokenized assets are reducing counterparty risk and freeing capital faster

• Successful programs treat people, training, and process as seriously as code and nodes

• Measured pilots with clear metrics create the momentum for broader transformation

---

Reflection Questions

1. Where do time, trust, or transparency create real friction in your organization today

2. Which single workflow could you upgrade first to prove value with a shared ledger and smart contracts

3. What data standards, identity models, and interoperability requirements would allow your partners to participate

4. How will you measure success in terms of time saved, errors avoided, or capital freed

5. What training and change management will help teams adopt the new system without disruption

Chapter 19

The Shift: From Quiet Integration to Global Transformation

Before we move into the macro changes blockchain is enabling, this chapter reorients the reader to think bigger, beyond industries, into economies, systems, and identity itself.

The most profound technological revolutions rarely announce themselves with fireworks. They seep quietly into the background, becoming part of our daily lives before we realize they have fundamentally reshaped the way the world operates. Blockchain is no longer a niche experiment discussed only in tech circles. Blockchain is the foundational layer being embedded into the systems that govern trade, finance, identity, trust, and every sector where transparency, security, and efficiency are essential. This chapter reorients the reader to see blockchain not as a tool for industries, but as an infrastructure for economies, governance, and human connection on a global scale.

The change is not simply about technology replacing older tools. It is about a deep restructuring of how economies function, how power is distributed, and how value is defined. What began as an alternative way to move digital currency has matured into a global architecture for transparent, secure, and efficient coordination. The shift is underway, and its trajectory is moving from quiet integration to global transformation.

According to a 2024 World Economic Forum report, over 91 percent of surveyed central banks are actively exploring or implementing blockchain-based systems for payments, settlements, and cross-border currency exchange. The International Monetary Fund has noted that tokenized assets, central bank digital currencies, and blockchain-powered payment rails are converging into what may become the most significant reconfiguration of the financial system since the introduction of the internet.

From Early Pilots to Global Infrastructure

In the early 2010s, blockchain was treated as an experiment, something to be tested in controlled environments. Now, the largest financial institutions in the world, including JPMorgan Chase, HSBC, and BNP Paribas, operate blockchain-powered platforms for settlement, trade finance, and cross-border transfers.

A 2023 Bank for International Settlements study confirmed that blockchain systems have reduced settlement times for international transactions from several days to a matter of seconds in pilot programs involving multiple G20 economies. These are no longer theoretical discussions. They are live systems processing billions of dollars in real value each week.

One notable example is Singapore's Project Ubin, which started as a central bank research initiative and evolved into a multi-industry platform for cross-border payments, asset tokenization, and regulatory compliance. Similarly, the

European Central Bank's experiments with the Digital Euro have moved into advanced testing phases, involving both retail and wholesale transaction models.

Beyond Finance: The Expansion into Global Systems

While finance has led the way, the transformation extends far beyond banks and payment processors. In 2024, the United Nations deployed blockchain to verify climate data submissions from member states, ensuring transparency and reducing the risk of falsified reporting. The World Food Programme has scaled its blockchain-based aid distribution system, Building Blocks, to deliver assistance to millions of people without requiring bank accounts or physical cash.

According to a joint study by the Massachusetts Institute of Technology and Stanford University, blockchain-based supply chain systems have improved traceability by over 60 percent in industries ranging from pharmaceuticals to luxury goods. This means life-saving medicines can be tracked from manufacturer to patient, counterfeit goods can be intercepted, and ethical sourcing claims can be independently verified.

The Identity Layer

Perhaps the most transformative application of blockchain is emerging in digital identity. The World Bank estimates that over 850 million people globally lack any form of legal identification, limiting their ability to access healthcare, education, or financial services.

Countries such as Estonia, with its e-Residency program, have already demonstrated how blockchain-secured identity can streamline everything from voting to business registration. In Sierra Leone, blockchain is being used to record citizens' identities securely, enabling them to participate in elections and access government programs for the first time.

This identity layer also addresses critical security concerns in the digital age. With blockchain, identity credentials can be verified without storing sensitive personal data in vulnerable central databases, reducing the risk of massive data breaches.

Economies in Transition

The macroeconomic implications of blockchain integration are substantial. The Organization for Economic Co-operation and Development (OECD) has highlighted blockchain's ability to increase GDP growth by enhancing trade efficiency, reducing corruption, and enabling microeconomic participation at scale.

In developing economies, blockchain can bypass legacy systems entirely, allowing nations to leapfrog directly into modern infrastructure. For example, in Nigeria, blockchain-based payment platforms are enabling small businesses to participate in global commerce without the friction of currency conversion or cross-border banking restrictions.

In advanced economies, blockchain is increasingly seen as the infrastructure layer for the "Internet of Value," enabling money, assets, and data to move with the same speed and reliability as information moves today.

Trust as the New Currency

At the core of this transformation is a redefinition of trust. According to a 2024 Harvard Business School working paper, the transparency of blockchain systems increases consumer and institutional trust, which in turn accelerates adoption rates across industries. When participants can verify transactions independently, trust shifts from intermediaries to the system itself.

This changes how individuals, corporations, and governments perceive and manage risk. It redefines accountability. And it creates a new expectation: if a process can be made transparent, it should be.

The Road Ahead

We are moving toward a world where blockchain is as invisible, and as indispensable, as the underlying protocols of the internet. The global transformation will not happen in a single moment. It will unfold in waves, industry by industry, region by region, until the infrastructure of trust itself has been rebuilt.

For policymakers, the challenge is to balance innovation with regulation, ensuring that blockchain's potential for empowerment is not overshadowed by misuse. For institutions, the challenge is to adopt early enough to remain competitive, while investing in the skills and systems needed to operate in a blockchain-driven economy. For individuals, the opportunity lies in understanding and engaging with these systems now, before they become so deeply embedded that opting out is no longer an option.

We are no longer asking whether blockchain will change the world. The question is how far-reaching, how fast, and how well we will navigate the transformation already in motion.

Key Takeaways

• Blockchain has shifted from experimental pilots to foundational infrastructure across finance, identity, and global systems.

• Academic and institutional research consistently confirms blockchain's ability to increase efficiency, transparency, and trust in high-stakes environments.

• Real-world deployments by central banks, the United Nations, and global corporations demonstrate that blockchain is now operating at scale.

• Digital identity solutions have the potential to include hundreds of millions of previously unregistered individuals in the global economy.

• The transformation is economic, technological, and cultural, redefining how trust is created and maintained.

Reflection Questions

1. Which current systems in your country or industry could be most improved by blockchain-level transparency and efficiency?

2. How might blockchain-based digital identity change access to services in underserved populations?

3. What steps can governments, institutions, and individuals take to ensure this transformation benefits the widest possible range of people?

Part 3

The Future of Decentralization and the Global Economy

Where blockchain is taking us next, and why it matters for everyone.

Chapter 20

The Surprising History Behind Two of Today's Most Powerful Technologies: Blockchain and AI

How Blockchain and AI Took Decades to Become Overnight Successes.

Most people think of blockchain and artificial intelligence (AI) as brand-new innovations. But neither of them is new. In fact, both technologies have been decades in the making, evolving behind the scenes through academic research, government programs, and private sector innovation.

Understanding where they came from helps us better understand where they are going. It also busts one of the biggest myths: blockchain and AI are passing trends. They are foundational technologies quietly transforming the systems we rely on such as finance, healthcare, identity, governance, education, and more.

A Quiet Revolution: The Origins of AI

The roots of artificial intelligence go back to the 1950s. Alan Turing, the British mathematician known for cracking Nazi codes during World War II, famously asked the question: "Can machines think?" In 1950, he developed what is now known as the Turing Test, a way to evaluate whether a machine's behavior is indistinguishable from a human's.

The term "artificial intelligence" was coined in 1956 at the Dartmouth Conference, organized by computer scientist John McCarthy. This event brought together some of the biggest minds of the time from Harvard, MIT, IBM, and Bell Labs. The

U.S. government funded much of this early research, seeing AI as a national defense asset during the Cold War.

Over the decades, AI evolved through cycles of enthusiasm and setbacks known as "AI winters," periods where funding dried up due to slow progress. But behind the scenes, core foundations were being laid.

DARPA and U.S. Government Involvement

Few institutions have shaped AI like DARPA, the U.S. Defense Advanced Research Projects Agency. Created in 1958 in response to the Soviet Union's launch of Sputnik, DARPA has been behind some of the most important digital innovations in history, including the internet (ARPANET), GPS, speech recognition, machine learning, and autonomous systems.

In the 1970s and 1980s, DARPA funded expert systems, early AI tools that mimicked human decision making for military and scientific applications. These systems were used in projects like MYCIN (developed at Stanford to diagnose bacterial infections) and XCON (used by Digital Equipment Corporation to configure complex computer systems). Though limited, these systems demonstrated AI's ability to support decisions in real world scenarios, from medical treatment to logistics planning.

By the 2000s, DARPA supported breakthroughs in natural language processing, robotics, and neural networks, paving the way for autonomous vehicles and systems like Siri and ChatGPT. DARPA's Urban Challenge in 2007 pushed the development of self-driving cars, a foundation for today's autonomous vehicle industry.

Universities and Tech Giants: Pioneering AI's Future

Alongside government efforts, universities like MIT, Stanford, Carnegie Mellon, and Oxford have been leading AI research since the beginning. MIT's AI Lab (founded in 1959) and Stanford's AI Lab (SAIL) produced generations of talent and technology that seeded today's biggest tech companies.

By the 2010s, with the rise of big data and cloud computing, AI exploded. Companies like Google, Facebook, Microsoft, and Amazon began integrating AI into their core products including search engines, recommendation systems, voice assistants, and more.

Today, AI powers everything from fraud detection to medical diagnostics to writing assistants, and it is only accelerating.

The Origin of Blockchain: More Than Just Bitcoin

While AI began with mathematical theory and government backed research, blockchain started as a decentralized solution to a different problem: a way to exchange value or verify information without middlemen.

The foundational concept of blockchain dates back to 1991, when Stuart Haber and W. Scott Stornetta introduced a method for time stamping digital documents in a way that could not be altered. In 1992, they added Merkle trees to improve the efficiency of the system and allow several documents to be collected into one block. Their work laid the groundwork for what would later evolve into blockchain technology.

Between 1991 and 2008, interest in secure, tamper proof digital ledgers grew steadily, especially in academic and cryptographic circles. In 1998, Wei Dai introduced the concept of "b money."

In 2004, Hal Finney (who would later receive the first ever Bitcoin transaction) developed Reusable Proof of Work, a key precursor to blockchain's consensus mechanisms. This was a system to prevent double spending in digital currency.

These developments influenced what would become Bitcoin.

NSA and Blockchain Like Concepts

In 1996, the National Security Agency (NSA) published a research paper titled "How to Make a Mint: The Cryptography of Anonymous Electronic Cash."

It proposed one of the earliest documented systems resembling blockchain:

- Double spending prevention
- Decentralized and anonymous, yet verifiable, transactions
- Public and private key cryptography
- Digital cash systems without a central issuer

This was 13 years before Bitcoin, and many consider it a blueprint for the cryptographic structure used in blockchain today.

The document was declassified and distributed by the NSA's Office of Information Security Research and Technology. Though the authorship was attributed to "Tatsuaki Okamoto, David Chaum, and others," its ideas would echo in Satoshi Nakamoto's white paper more than a decade later.

In 2008, Satoshi Nakamoto published the Bitcoin white paper, combining these ideas into a peer-to-peer currency built on a blockchain. By 2009, the first Bitcoin was mined, and history was made.

Fun fact: Satoshi Nakamoto referenced Wei Dai's b money in the original Bitcoin white paper published in 2008.

Government and Enterprise Involvement in Blockchain

At first, blockchain was dismissed as fringe tech. But governments and corporations quickly saw its potential, not just for currency, but for identity management, supply chain transparency, secure data exchange, and smart contracts. Here is how that unfolded:

- 2014 to 2016: The U.S. Department of Homeland Security, Food and Drug Administration (FDA), and Department of Defense began exploring blockchain to secure data, improve logistics, and enhance cybersecurity for national infrastructure. DHS awarded grants to startups like Factom to test blockchain's use in border security and digital identity.
- IBM, Walmart, and Maersk began piloting blockchain solutions for supply chains around 2016. IBM's Food Trust platform, for example, was used by Walmart to trace leafy greens in seconds, a task that once took days. Maersk used blockchain to digitize shipping documentation, reducing fraud and accelerating global trade.

  • Around the same time, JPMorgan Chase launched Quorum, an enterprise focused blockchain platform that built on Ethereum's technology to serve financial institutions with faster, private, and permissioned transactions.

• Visa, Mastercard, and PayPal began experimenting with blockchain for cross border payments and stablecoin settlements. Visa introduced its B2B Connect platform in 2019 to simplify international business payments using distributed ledger technology.

• The World Economic Forum (WEF), through its Centre for the Fourth Industrial Revolution, initiated programs using blockchain for humanitarian aid delivery, digital identity verification for displaced persons, and climate accountability tracking, aiming to make aid more transparent and efficient.

A Global Effort

While the U.S. played a dominant early role, it is important to recognize the global nature of these technologies:

• The United Arab Emirates has quietly established itself as one of the main global players. Dubai's Virtual Assets Regulatory Authority has created a transparent regulatory environment for digital assets, while Abu Dhabi Global Market has launched world leading blockchain and AI initiatives. The UAE is not following, it is positioning itself as a central hub where global capital, blockchain ecosystems, and AI innovation converge. Its vision stretches across finance, energy, real estate, and even space technology, signaling an ambition to define the future from the desert outward.

• Canada led AI breakthroughs through researchers like Geoffrey Hinton, who helped advance deep learning and neural networks.

• China has invested heavily in AI for surveillance, smart cities, and its digital yuan, while also becoming a leader in blockchain patents.

• The European Union established the European Blockchain Services Infrastructure (EBSI) to support cross border public services and is leading in AI regulation for ethical use.

• India uses blockchain in public welfare and land records and is rapidly scaling its AI infrastructure across education and healthcare.

• Switzerland, home to the "Crypto Valley," has become a major blockchain hub for innovation and regulation.

Why This Matters Now

Both AI and blockchain are exploding into the mainstream at the same time, not by coincidence, but because the world has caught up to the technology.

They solve different problems:

- AI helps us process massive amounts of data, simulate human behavior, and automate complex decisions.
- Blockchain gives us a way to securely record, verify, and share that data without needing to trust a centralized authority.

Together, they are reshaping how we work, live, govern, and grow.

The Future: AI and Blockchain Are Converging

We are now entering a phase where AI and blockchain no longer operate in separate lanes. They work together.

AI can analyze blockchain data for fraud detection, pattern recognition, and predictive analytics. Blockchain adds transparency and integrity to AI processes, ensuring model training is ethical and results are verifiable.

They Are Not the Future, They Are the Foundation

If there is one thing to take away, it is this:

Blockchain and AI are not speculative trends. They are not emerging. They have emerged.

Their histories are rich. Their development spans generations. And their future will shape everything, from the way we govern, educate, and grow businesses, to how we connect, earn, and evolve as individuals.

This is a transformation of the systems that is shaping our lives.

Key Takeaways

• Blockchain and AI have been decades in the making, not passing trends.

• Government institutions like DARPA and the NSA played pivotal roles in shaping early development.

• Major corporations including IBM, Walmart, JPMorgan, and Visa are deploying blockchain at scale.

• The UAE has emerged as a main global hub alongside China, India, the EU, and Switzerland.

• The convergence of blockchain and AI is creating systems of trust and intelligence that will transform economies and societies.

Reflection Questions

1. How does knowing the historical origins of blockchain and AI change your view of these technologies today?

2. Which global leader's strategy in blockchain or AI do you believe will have the greatest long-term impact?

3. How do you see the convergence of AI and blockchain influencing industries you interact with most?

4. What steps can you take to prepare yourself or your business for a future where these technologies are fully embedded in everyday life?

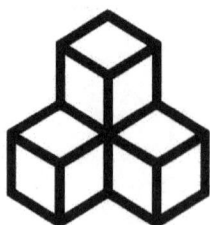

BLOCKCHAIN & AI

BUILT OVER GENERATIONS

FROM RESEARCH TO MAINSTREAM

DRIVING GLOBAL TRANSFORMATION

Chapter 21

Decentralized Identity: The New Standard for Trust and Privacy

Understand how decentralized identity gives individuals more control over their credentials, privacy, and digital presence.

Every interaction in the digital world begins with identity. Whether you are logging into your bank account, verifying your age to purchase alcohol, or applying for a new job, identity sits at the center. Yet, today's identity systems are built on outdated foundations. Personal information is scattered across countless centralized databases, each controlled by corporations, governments, or platforms that determine who gets access, how data is stored, and what happens when breaches occur.

The result is a fragile system filled with risk. Billions of records have been exposed in data breaches over the past decade, leading to identity theft, financial loss, and erosion of trust. Every time you create a new account or upload personal information, you are handing over control to an organization that may not protect it. Worse still, individuals have almost no say in how their identity is used, shared, or monetized.

Blockchain is introducing a new paradigm: decentralized identity, often called self-sovereign identity (SSI). It represents one of the most transformative shifts in how humans will prove who they are, access services, and protect their privacy in the digital age.

What Is Decentralized Identity?

Decentralized identity gives individuals the ability to own and manage their digital credentials without relying on a central authority. Instead of companies holding your data, you control it directly through secure, blockchain-based wallets.

A decentralized identity system typically consists of three elements:

- **Decentralized Identifiers (DIDs):** Unique identifiers created on a blockchain that belong to an individual, not a company.

- **Verifiable Credentials:** Digital proofs of identity, such as a driver's license, diploma, or professional certification, issued by trusted entities and cryptographically secured.

- **Digital Wallets:** Applications where individuals store and selectively share their credentials without revealing unnecessary personal data.

This framework flips the traditional model. Instead of showing your entire driver's license to prove you are over 21, you could share a cryptographic proof that verifies your age and nothing more. You remain in control of who sees what.

Why Centralized Identity Is Broken

The current identity system is built around silos. Each company creates its own login system, and each institution stores your personal records on centralized servers. This leads to:

- Massive data breaches: Equifax, LinkedIn, Facebook, and many others have exposed millions of users.

- Inconsistent access: You juggle dozens of usernames and passwords across services.

- Overexposure of information: To prove something simple like age or citizenship, you often reveal far more information than necessary.

- Lack of portability: If you change employers, schools, or platforms, your identity does not move with you.

Decentralized identity addresses all of these issues by removing central intermediaries and giving individuals direct control.

How Blockchain Enables Self-Sovereign Identity

Blockchain serves as the trust layer for decentralized identity. Instead of relying on a company to maintain a record, the blockchain provides a tamper-proof, verifiable ledger. This ensures that identities cannot be altered, revoked, or faked without consensus.

Key benefits include:

- **Security:** Credentials are cryptographically secured and nearly impossible to forge.

- **Portability:** Your identity moves with you across platforms, jobs, and countries.

- **Selective disclosure:** You reveal only the information necessary for a given interaction.

- **Interoperability:** Standards like W3C's Decentralized Identifiers (DIDs) ensure global compatibility.

The role of blockchain is not to store your private data directly but to act as the verification layer that ensures authenticity. Your personal data remains in your control, often stored locally in your wallet.

Real-World Examples of Decentralized Identity in Action

- **Sweden's BankID:** Used by more than 8 million citizens, this digital identity system enables secure authentication and signatures across financial services, healthcare, and government platforms.

- **Microsoft Entra (formerly Azure Active Directory + ION project):** Microsoft has been pioneering decentralized identity through its ION network, built on top of Bitcoin. With Entra, enterprises can issue verifiable credentials that individuals control through their digital wallets.

- **IBM and Hyperledger Indy:** IBM has been developing decentralized identity solutions with Hyperledger, focusing on enterprise use cases like supply chains and employee verification.

- **European Union's eIDAS 2.0:** The EU is developing a European Digital Identity Wallet that will allow every citizen to securely prove credentials like age, qualifications, or licenses across all member states.

- **World Economic Forum pilots:** WEF has highlighted decentralized identity as critical infrastructure for global trade, finance, and cross-border travel.

- **Fintech adoption:** Banks and fintechs are exploring decentralized KYC (Know Your Customer) processes where customers can use blockchain-based credentials to verify themselves instantly without repeatedly uploading sensitive documents.

Everyday Scenarios Where Decentralized Identity Changes Lives

- **Finance:** Opening a bank account, applying for a loan, or getting approved for a mortgage can be done instantly by presenting verifiable credentials without uploading sensitive documents multiple times.

- **Travel:** Imagine crossing borders without passports filled with personal details. Instead, you present a verifiable credential stored in your wallet, recognized globally.

- **Healthcare:** You control your medical history, selectively sharing records with doctors or insurers without fear of data leaks.

- **Education:** Diplomas and certifications are issued as verifiable credentials, eliminating fake degrees and streamlining job applications.

- **Workplace:** Instead of filling out endless onboarding paperwork, employees share blockchain-secured credentials proving their qualifications and right-to-work status.

- **Commerce:** Online shopping no longer requires exposing credit card numbers or home addresses unnecessarily. Proof of authorization is enough.

Why Privacy and Trust Are Central

In a world of constant data leaks, privacy has become a form of currency. Individuals demand greater control over their digital presence, and decentralized identity provides exactly that. It restores trust in digital interactions by ensuring authenticity without overexposure.

For businesses, adopting decentralized identity is not just about compliance. It reduces the liability of storing customer data while improving user experience. Instead of being a gatekeeper, companies become verifiers of trust.

Challenges to Adoption

Despite the promise, decentralized identity faces hurdles:

- **Standardization:** Competing frameworks and lack of universal adoption slow progress.

- **User experience:** Wallets and cryptographic keys must be simple enough for everyday users.

- **Regulatory alignment:** Governments must balance privacy with security requirements like AML (anti-money laundering).

- **Trust anchors:** Adoption requires trusted issuers like governments, universities, and banks to provide verifiable credentials.

These challenges are real but solvable. Much like the early internet, once momentum builds, adoption will accelerate rapidly.

The Future of Decentralized Identity

Decentralized identity will become the new backbone of trust in a digital-first world. As artificial intelligence, the metaverse, and immersive digital environments expand, proving who we are will become essential. Bots and deepfakes already blur the lines of authenticity. A cryptographically verifiable identity ensures humans can distinguish truth from manipulation.

By 2030, it is likely that digital wallets holding self-sovereign credentials will be as common as smartphones today. Just as you cannot function in modern society without email or banking apps, decentralized identity will become a baseline requirement for participation in global commerce, education, and governance.

Key Takeaways

- Decentralized identity gives individuals control of their credentials, privacy, and digital presence.

- Blockchain enables verifiable, tamper-proof credentials without relying on centralized authorities.

- Major companies and governments are already piloting decentralized identity frameworks, including Microsoft, IBM, Sweden, Estonia, and the EU.

- Everyday scenarios like travel, healthcare, finance, and employment will be transformed by verifiable credentials.

- Adoption challenges remain, but decentralized identity is set to become the new global standard for trust.

Reflection Questions

1. How much control do you currently feel you have over your digital identity?

2. Which parts of your personal data would you want to manage through a secure wallet?

3. How would decentralized identity change the way you interact with businesses, schools, or governments?

4. What risks do you see in continuing with centralized identity systems in the coming decade?

5. How could decentralized identity protect you from identity theft, fraud, or overexposure of personal information?

Chapter 22

DAOs: Redefining Ownership, Governance, and Global Collaboration

DAOs are reshaping how people build, own, and govern organizations without traditional hierarchies or borders.

For centuries, organizations have been defined by hierarchies. Leaders sat at the top of pyramids, decisions flowed downward, and members had limited influence unless they held power. The rise of Decentralized Autonomous Organizations, or DAOs, is transforming this model at its core. Instead of relying on centralized authority, DAOs operate on blockchain networks where rules are encoded into smart contracts, and members collectively participate in decision making. This approach redefines what it means to build, own, and govern a community, a company, or even an entire global initiative.

DAOs strip away borders, bureaucracy, and the limitations of geography. A developer in Argentina, an artist in Nigeria, and an investor in Singapore can all collaborate on the same project, with equal access to information and voting power. This kind of global, digitally native governance structure is rapidly gaining momentum.

What Makes a DAO Different

The heart of a DAO lies in two things: transparency and shared control. In traditional organizations, decisions often happen behind closed doors, with layers of management influencing outcomes. In a DAO, every proposal, vote, and allocation of funds is recorded on the blockchain for members to see. Rules are coded into smart contracts, which automatically enforce outcomes without needing a central authority.

Ownership also works differently. Instead of shares issued by a company, members hold tokens that represent both their stake and their voting rights. These tokens give them a voice in governance and a financial incentive to see the project succeed. The more engaged the community, the stronger the DAO becomes.

This creates a balance between contribution and reward. Members are not passive stakeholders but active participants in shaping direction. In many DAOs, one token equals one vote, though other models weight influence based on participation or reputation.

Everyday Impact and Possibilities

Imagine an artist collective where every member has a say in which projects to fund and how profits are distributed. Or consider a group of freelancers pooling resources into a shared treasury, with automated rules for distributing payments fairly. Even real estate investment can be reshaped when global contributors fund and co-own a property through a DAO, earning returns proportionate to their stake.

Financial systems are also being reshaped by DAOs. Investment clubs can form without requiring a central fund manager. Communities can create mutual aid networks where funds are automatically distributed to members in need based on predefined rules. Sports fans can come together to own parts of teams, athletes, or facilities. What was once reserved for the wealthy or well-connected can now be built by communities themselves.

Real World Examples

Some DAOs are already reshaping entire industries:

- **MakerDAO**: One of the earliest and most influential DAOs, MakerDAO manages the DAI stablecoin, ensuring its peg to the US dollar through community-driven governance. Members vote on risk parameters, collateral types, and protocol updates. It has become one of the cornerstones of decentralized finance.

- **Uniswap DAO**: Uniswap, a leading decentralized exchange, is governed by a DAO where UNI token holders propose and vote on upgrades, treasury usage, and ecosystem development. Its governance decisions directly shape the future of one of the most widely used financial protocols in the blockchain world.

- **CityDAO in Wyoming**: Pioneering real-world integration, CityDAO bought land in Wyoming and put ownership and governance into the hands of its DAO members. They experiment with new forms of landownership, zoning, and municipal decision making, offering a glimpse into how physical communities might be governed in the future.

- **ConstitutionDAO**: In 2021, a group of strangers on the internet came together to raise over $40 million in less than a week to bid on a copy of the U.S. Constitution at auction. While they did not win, their speed, scale, and ability to coordinate demonstrated the raw potential of DAOs as a new organizational force.

These examples show that DAOs are more than experimental, they are already managing billions of dollars and coordinating global communities at scale.

Challenges and Growing Pains

Like any new system, DAOs face hurdles. Scalability can be difficult, as thousands of members may struggle to reach consensus quickly. Voter participation is often low, with only a fraction of token holders actively voting, which risks concentrating power in the hands of a few. Security is another issue. Smart contract vulnerabilities can be exploited, as seen in the infamous 2016 DAO hack that led to Ethereum's first major split.

That hack targeted a decentralized investment fund called *The DAO*, which had pooled over $150 million worth of Ether from thousands of contributors. A flaw in its smart contract code allowed an attacker to siphon away about one-third of the funds into a separate account. This crisis forced the Ethereum community to face a defining choice: intervene to recover the stolen funds or uphold the principle that "code is law" and leave the hack untouched.

The disagreement resulted in a hard fork, or permanent division, of the blockchain. One chain, Ethereum (ETH), chose to restore the stolen funds. The other, Ethereum Classic (ETC), refused to alter history, keeping the hack intact. This "split" was proof that decentralized systems are not governed by code alone but by the collective values and choices of their communities. It raised lasting questions about how much intervention should exist in a supposedly immutable system, and who gets to make that call.

There are also questions of legal recognition. Traditional laws are designed around centralized corporations, and while some jurisdictions like Wyoming and Switzerland have begun recognizing DAOs as legal entities, many governments have yet to adapt. Until there is global clarity, DAOs exist in a gray area between community cooperatives and experimental digital companies.

Still, these challenges are not barriers but steppingstones. Just as the early internet faced issues of regulation, trust, and adoption, DAOs are working through their own growing pains. The communities that solve these challenges will shape the next generation of global collaboration.

Why DAOs Matter

The significance of DAOs extends far beyond blockchain enthusiasts. They represent a reimagining of human collaboration at a scale we have never seen before. DAOs are not simply about voting or managing treasuries. They are about enabling people anywhere to create shared value, without needing to rely on centralized institutions.

In a world where many feel disconnected from traditional systems of power, DAOs offer transparency, accountability, and ownership. They give individuals the ability to shape outcomes directly rather than waiting for leaders to act. Whether for art, finance, activism, or civic life, DAOs show us what is possible when technology empowers collective intelligence.

The Road Ahead

As DAOs evolve, expect them to move beyond the niche world of crypto into mainstream industries. Entertainment companies may use DAOs to let fans influence storylines or production choices. Global nonprofits may adopt DAO structures to ensure transparent use of donations. Even governments may experiment with DAO-like models for citizen participation in local decisions.

The trajectory is clear: DAOs are a new framework for ownership and governance, one that unlocks the power of communities to create and manage value together.

Key Takeaways

- DAOs replace centralized hierarchies with community-driven governance on blockchain networks.

- Token ownership provides both financial stake and voting rights, making members active participants.

- Real-world DAOs like MakerDAO, Uniswap DAO, and CityDAO are already managing billions and experimenting with new models.

- Challenges include voter participation, security, and legal recognition, but solutions are emerging.

- DAOs are paving the way for borderless, transparent, and inclusive collaboration.

Reflection Questions

1. How might DAOs reshape industries you are part of or connected to today?

2. What communities in your life could benefit from transparent, decentralized decision making?

3. How do DAOs challenge your current understanding of ownership and governance?

4. What role would you personally want to play in a DAO, investor, builder, voter, or strategist?

CHAPTER 23

The Token Economy: How Incentivized Networks Are Changing Business

Tokens are the new building blocks of digital economies, fueling participation, loyalty, and innovation across sectors.

Tokens are the fuel powering entire digital economies, shifting how people interact with platforms, how businesses grow, and how value circulates across global networks. Unlike traditional loyalty points or reward systems, tokens are programmable, transferable, and integrated into decentralized systems, enabling new forms of participation, ownership, and collaboration. They represent not just financial assets, but new ways of structuring relationships between companies and communities.

The Rise of Token Incentives

Incentives have always driven human behavior. Airlines reward frequent flyers with miles, coffee shops offer loyalty cards, and credit cards entice customers with cash back. Tokens take these models and amplify them with technology. A token can be instantly transferred to another person, traded on an exchange, or used to access services. The underlying blockchain ensures transparency and scarcity, giving tokens a trust foundation that traditional loyalty systems lack.

This shift means that incentives are no longer isolated to one company's ecosystem. They are portable across industries, globally accessible, and in many cases, liquid. A user who earns a token from contributing to a decentralized platform can sell it, use it in another app, or hold it as a stake in the future growth of the network.

Utility, Governance, and Security Tokens

The token economy is diverse, and not all tokens serve the same purpose.

- **Utility tokens** give access to a product or service. For example, Filecoin's token powers a decentralized storage marketplace. Users pay with Filecoin to store data, while providers earn tokens for contributing storage space.

- **Governance tokens** allow holders to vote on the future of a project. Uniswap, one of the largest decentralized exchanges, gives governance rights to UNI token holders, who influence decisions ranging from fee structures to protocol upgrades.

- **Security tokens** represent regulated financial assets like equity or bonds. These are increasingly being explored by institutions, as they combine blockchain's efficiency with the safeguards of traditional securities law.

Understanding these categories is critical because they shape how networks are built and how participants engage.

Tokens in Consumer Engagement

One of the clearest areas where tokens are transforming business is in customer engagement. Instead of passive consumers, users become stakeholders. Brands like Starbucks have experimented with tokenized loyalty programs that go beyond points. In 2022, Starbucks launched Odyssey, a blockchain-powered rewards system using digital collectibles to grant experiences and perks. Customers are no longer just drinking coffee, they are holding a digital asset tied to the brand, one that can be resold or traded.

This model introduces a feedback loop of engagement. Customers are rewarded not only for purchases but also for their participation in the brand's ecosystem. Sharing content, attending events, or interacting with communities can all be tied to token rewards, driving deeper loyalty.

Tokenized Networks in Action

Real world examples are rapidly growing:

- **Helium** built a decentralized wireless network by rewarding individuals with tokens for setting up hotspots. Instead of a telecom giant shouldering infrastructure costs, thousands of individuals contributed to the network, each incentivized by token earnings.

- **Brave Browser** introduced the Basic Attention Token (BAT), paying users for viewing ads and allowing them to tip creators directly. This flipped the traditional advertising model on its head, aligning incentives among advertisers, users, and creators.

- **Reddit** experimented with Community Points, allowing users to earn tokens for valuable contributions in certain subreddits, creating micro-economies inside the platform.

These examples highlight how tokens make it possible for networks to scale faster and more efficiently by directly aligning user incentives with platform growth.

Corporate and Institutional Integration

Tokens are no longer confined to startups or experimental projects. Large corporations and financial institutions are entering the token economy. BlackRock, the world's largest asset manager, has spoken publicly about the potential of tokenization to reshape financial markets by making assets like real estate, bonds, and equities easier to trade. JPMorgan has already tested token-based settlement systems for cross-border payments.

Even luxury brands are experimenting. Gucci and Louis Vuitton have explored blockchain-based tokens to verify authenticity of products, reducing counterfeits and enhancing consumer trust. These tokens act as digital certificates of ownership, combining brand prestige with blockchain transparency.

Token Economies and Network Effects

Tokens succeed when they create network effects, the more people who use them, the more valuable they become. Consider Bitcoin. Its growth is not just due to its technical foundation but because millions of people, companies, and institutions now hold and transact with it. The value of the network increases as adoption spreads, creating a self-reinforcing cycle.

For businesses, token-driven network effects can turn customers into marketers and participants into builders. A ride-sharing app that rewards drivers and passengers with tokens not only improves adoption but also distributes ownership of the ecosystem across its users.

Challenges and Risks

The token economy is powerful, but it also comes with risks. Volatility can make tokens difficult to use as stable incentives. Over time, stablecoins and other mechanisms have emerged to solve this, but many tokens still experience rapid price swings. Regulatory clarity is another major challenge. In some countries, tokens are seen as securities and subject to strict laws. In others, they operate in a gray zone, leaving businesses uncertain about compliance.

Speculative behavior can also undermine the utility of tokens. Projects designed for long-term use can be hijacked by traders looking for quick profits, creating unsustainable bubbles. For tokens to thrive, they must strike a balance between incentivizing participation and maintaining long-term value.

The Future of Tokenized Economies

Looking ahead, tokens are set to become as common as websites or apps. They will underpin not just consumer loyalty but entire financial and social systems. Governments are exploring tokenized public services, where citizens earn tokens for sustainable behavior or civic engagement. Universities could issue tokens for completed courses, creating verifiable credentials. Healthcare systems might reward healthy habits with tokenized incentives that reduce insurance costs.

The greatest promise of tokens lies in their ability to align incentives across diverse groups. By making participation both meaningful and valuable, tokens open the door to economies that are more inclusive, transparent, and adaptable to global challenges.

Key Takeaways

- Tokens are programmable incentives that extend far beyond traditional loyalty programs.

- Utility, governance, and security tokens serve different roles within digital economies.

- Real-world examples like Helium, Brave, and Starbucks Odyssey show how tokens are transforming business models.

- Corporations and institutions are increasingly integrating tokenization into finance, retail, and luxury goods.

- Token economies thrive on network effects but must navigate challenges like volatility, speculation, and regulation.

- The future of tokens spans industries from education to healthcare, aligning incentives in new and powerful ways.

Reflection Questions

1. How might tokens reshape loyalty programs in industries you are most familiar with?

2. What role do you see governance tokens playing in the businesses of the future?

3. How could token-based incentives make you more engaged with a company, platform, or community?

4. What risks do you think must be addressed before tokens can become part of everyday life?

CHAPTER 24

How Blockchain Enables Borderless Economies and Digital Nations

Blockchain is eliminating the limitations of geography, enabling new forms of citizenship, trade, and participation without borders.

For most of human history, your birthplace determined your opportunities. Citizenship, trade access, and financial inclusion were all tied to geography. Borders defined who you could do business with, which institutions you could trust, and how freely you could move across systems. But blockchain is rewriting this story. It is giving rise to borderless economies and even the beginnings of digital nations, where participation depends not on where you live but on whether you are connected.

What once seemed like science fiction is becoming a lived reality. Communities are forming online with their own currencies, governance systems, and collective resources. Entrepreneurs are incorporating businesses that span continents without physical headquarters. Citizens of developing countries are gaining access to the same financial rails as those in the world's largest economies. Geography still matters for culture and local governance, but it no longer locks people out of global participation.

The Rise of Borderless Economies

Blockchain provides a neutral infrastructure that is not owned by any single government or corporation. This neutrality allows economic activity to flourish across borders in ways that were impossible with legacy systems.

Consider remittances, the flow of money sent home by migrant workers. Traditionally, these transfers relied on intermediaries like Western Union or banks, often carrying fees as high as 10 percent and delays of several days. Today, blockchain-based payments allow workers in the United States to send funds to families in the Philippines or Nigeria in seconds at a fraction of the cost. For households dependent on remittances, this shift is transformative.

Decentralized finance (DeFi) platforms take the idea further. They allow anyone with an internet connection to lend, borrow, or earn interest on digital assets without needing approval from a bank. A farmer in rural Kenya or a student in Brazil can access the same financial products as a Silicon Valley entrepreneur. Borders do not disappear, but they lose their power to determine who participates.

Digital Nations and New Forms of Citizenship

Beyond finance, blockchain is enabling new experiments in governance and identity. Entire communities are declaring themselves as digital nations. These entities may not yet have seats at the United Nations, but they are creating frameworks for citizenship, rights, and responsibilities that operate independently of geography.

One of the most well-known examples is Estonia's e-Residency program. While Estonia is a physical nation, it has pioneered a digital model that allows anyone in the world to apply for e-residency. Holders can open European Union bank accounts, incorporate businesses, and sign digital contracts, all without setting foot in the country. Blockchain and secure digital IDs form the backbone of this system.

Another example is Bitnation, an early attempt to create a borderless digital nation where citizens could form contracts, resolve disputes, and govern themselves using blockchain protocols. Though experimental, projects like Bitnation reveal the growing desire for digital-first citizenship.

Real-World Stories of Borderless Impact

- **Nigeria and Crypto Adoption**: With currency volatility eroding local savings, Nigerian entrepreneurs and citizens have turned to stablecoins like USDT and USDC for everyday transactions. Blockchain has become a lifeline, enabling participation in the global economy despite instability in the local financial system.

- **El Salvador's Bitcoin Initiative**: In 2021, El Salvador became the first nation to adopt Bitcoin as legal tender. While controversial, it marked a symbolic shift: a small nation using blockchain to assert independence from legacy global financial structures.

- **The United Arab Emirates and Global Hubs**: The UAE has positioned itself as a hub for blockchain-driven economies. Dubai's Virtual Assets Regulatory Authority and Abu Dhabi Global Market have established frameworks that attract companies building borderless platforms. Entrepreneurs from every continent are incorporating businesses in the UAE to access global markets.

Everyday Scenarios of Borderless Living

The power of blockchain-enabled economies can be felt in everyday life:

- **Employment**: A freelance designer in Argentina can receive instant payment from a client in Germany through stablecoin transfers, avoiding the friction of international banking.

- **Education**: A student in Indonesia can enroll in an online course, pay tuition in cryptocurrency, and receive a verifiable digital diploma recognized worldwide.

- **Healthcare**: A patient traveling between India and Singapore can share blockchain-secured medical records instantly with doctors in both countries.

- **Commerce**: Small businesses can reach global buyers through tokenized platforms that ensure authenticity of goods and reduce reliance on intermediaries.

Challenges to Borderless Economies

While the promise is enormous, challenges remain.

- **Regulation**: Governments are cautious about borderless systems that bypass traditional controls. Efforts like the European Union's MiCA framework and U.S. Treasury guidance show attempts to bring blockchain within regulatory scope.

- **Inequality of Access**: Internet connectivity and digital literacy remain uneven. Without addressing infrastructure gaps, blockchain risks reinforcing divides.

- **Sovereignty Concerns**: Nations fear the erosion of their ability to control monetary policy, taxation, and identity when citizens engage in borderless systems.

- **Trust and Adoption**: Like the early internet, blockchain economies must prove reliability at scale before they become truly mainstream.

Looking Ahead: Toward Digital Nations

The seeds of digital nations are already planted. By 2035, it is plausible that millions of people will hold dual identities: one tied to their geographic nation, and one tied to a borderless digital community. These digital nations may not replace states, but they will coexist, offering new layers of belonging, opportunity, and economic participation.

For businesses, this creates entirely new markets. For individuals, it means freedom to choose how and where they participate. For governments, it raises urgent questions about sovereignty, taxation, and the nature of citizenship in an increasingly digital-first world.

The shift is not about abandoning geography but about reducing its limitations. Borders will still matter for culture and governance, but they will no longer decide who gets access to opportunity. That power is shifting into the hands of individuals connected through blockchain.

Key Takeaways

- Blockchain is creating borderless economies by enabling instant, low-cost transactions across nations.

- Digital nations and e-residency programs show how identity and citizenship are evolving beyond geography.

- Countries like Nigeria, El Salvador, and the UAE highlight real-world experiments in borderless systems.

- Everyday scenarios such as payments, healthcare, and education are being redefined through blockchain-enabled global access.

- Challenges include regulation, infrastructure, and sovereignty, but the direction toward borderless participation is clear.

Reflection Questions

1. How might borderless economies change the opportunities available to you personally or professionally?

2. What risks do you see if governments resist or restrict blockchain-driven systems?

3. Could you imagine holding both a geographic passport and a digital citizenship, and how might that affect your sense of belonging?

4. How could businesses leverage borderless systems to reach new customers or communities?

5. What role should nations play in adapting to digital-first economies that operate beyond borders?

CHAPTER 25

Why Transparency Is the New Luxury: Blockchain in Luxury Goods

From designer handbags to fine art, blockchain is being used to verify authenticity and create new standards of trust in high-end markets.

Luxury has always been about more than price. From a Rolex watch to a Hermès Birkin bag, luxury signals rarity, craftsmanship, and heritage. Yet in today's world, exclusivity faces a growing challenge: counterfeiting. The global counterfeit market has exploded to more than half a trillion dollars annually, with luxury fashion, jewelry, and fine art among its biggest targets. Shoppers risk paying thousands for items that are fake, while brands lose revenue and reputation.

For consumers, trust has become the true luxury. Buyers want certainty that what they own is authentic, ethically sourced, and crafted to the standards the brand promises. This is where blockchain is stepping in. Luxury companies are turning to blockchain not just as a security tool, but as a way to elevate transparency into the ultimate expression of exclusivity.

Blockchain as the Digital Certificate of Authenticity

At its core, blockchain provides an incorruptible ledger of truth. For luxury, this translates into digital certificates of authenticity that cannot be forged or tampered with. Each handbag, watch, or piece of art can be issued a unique blockchain record at the point of creation.

That record contains details such as:

- Date and place of manufacture

- Materials used and supply chain data

- Ownership history across resales

- Proof of authenticity from the brand itself

Unlike paper certificates or QR codes that can be faked, blockchain records exist permanently across a decentralized network. This means that anyone, from a buyer in Paris to a reseller in Hong Kong, can verify instantly whether an item is real.

Real-World Adoption in Luxury

Several of the world's most prestigious luxury brands have already embraced blockchain.

LVMH (Louis Vuitton Moët Hennessy): LVMH, the parent company of Louis Vuitton, Dior, and other houses, launched the AURA blockchain consortium. It issues digital certificates of authenticity for high-end goods, allowing customers to track the full history of their purchase from production to store.

Prada and Cartier: Together with LVMH, Prada and Cartier co-founded the Aura Blockchain Consortium, setting industry-wide standards for authenticity and transparency.

De Beers: One of the most influential names in diamonds, De Beers uses blockchain through its platform Tracr to track stones from mine to market. This ensures that diamonds are ethically sourced and free from conflict, addressing one of the luxury sector's most sensitive issues.

Christie's and Blockchain in Fine Art:

Christie's, one of the world's most prestigious auction houses, has become a leader in integrating blockchain into the art market. In 2018, it partnered with Artory to record the sale of the Barney A. Ebsworth collection on blockchain, securing provenance and authenticity for over $300 million worth of modern American art. Since then, Christie's has continued to expand its blockchain use. In 2022, it launched additional provenance-verified auctions, and in 2024 it partnered with Kresus to issue blockchain-backed ownership certificates on the Base blockchain for photography auctions. By embedding blockchain into high-value sales, Christie's is addressing one of the art industry's biggest challenges, fraud and counterfeit works that cost billions annually, while giving collectors confidence that their acquisitions are both genuine and permanently verifiable.

Everyday Impact for Luxury Buyers

The transformation goes beyond elite buyers. For anyone considering a major luxury purchase, blockchain shifts the entire experience.

Imagine walking into a boutique in Milan and scanning a QR code that shows the verified blockchain record of the handbag you are holding. You can see where the leather came from, who crafted it, and confirm that no duplicate record exists. If you later decide to sell the bag, the blockchain record assures the next buyer that the piece is authentic, protecting its resale value.

Collectors can now verify ownership history instantly before purchasing secondhand pieces. In fine art, digital passports allow museums to track provenance without relying solely on paper records that can be misplaced or forged. Transparency itself has become a new form of luxury.

Why Luxury Consumers Value Transparency

The psychology of luxury has always revolved around trust and rarity. Blockchain strengthens both.

- **Proof of authenticity:** Buyers know they are getting the real thing.

- **Sustainability and ethics:** Modern consumers increasingly demand proof that their purchases are responsibly sourced. Blockchain enables brands to document supply chains with precision.

- **Resale value:** Verified ownership increases confidence in secondary markets, expanding demand and value.

- **Prestige of technology:** Owning blockchain-verified goods positions buyers as forward-thinking, aligning with the innovation prestige many luxury brands project.

Transparency is no longer a behind-the-scenes feature. It is now part of the brand story, a signal of exclusivity in itself.

The Challenges Ahead

Despite progress, challenges remain.

- **Adoption across the industry:** While major brands are leading, thousands of smaller luxury houses have not yet integrated blockchain.

- **Consumer education:** Many buyers do not yet understand blockchain, meaning its benefits must be communicated in simple, experiential ways.

- **Integration with resale markets:** Ensuring that resale platforms and secondary markets adopt these verification systems is essential for full impact.

- **Costs:** Implementing blockchain infrastructure can be expensive for brands, especially in industries with thin margins.

As these challenges are addressed, the industry is likely to move toward a future where every luxury product comes with a blockchain record by default.

Beyond Goods: The Future of Luxury Experiences

Luxury is expanding beyond physical goods into experiences. Blockchain is also playing a role here. Tokenized experiences, such as exclusive access to fashion shows, VIP events, or private sales, are being issued as non-fungible tokens (NFTs) tied to a buyer's verified identity. Owning not just a luxury item but a provable, exclusive experience has become the next standard of authenticity.

Fashion houses and luxury resorts are already using blockchain-based loyalty systems where ownership of digital assets unlocks exclusive privileges, private access, and once-unattainable experiences. This fusion of physical and digital luxury is not a passing experiment. It is the opening chapter of a new standard, where authenticity, transparency, and access are the true markers of value. What begins as innovation in luxury will soon ripple outward, reshaping how all industries define ownership and exclusivity in the decades ahead.

Key Takeaways

- Counterfeiting has made trust and transparency the ultimate luxuries in high-end markets.

- Blockchain provides permanent, tamper-proof certificates of authenticity for luxury goods.

- Leading brands like LVMH, Prada, Cartier, De Beers, and Vacheron Constantin are already using blockchain to secure provenance.

- Blockchain boosts not only authenticity but also sustainability, ethics, and resale value.

- The luxury industry is moving toward a future where every high-value item comes with blockchain verification, expanding into experiences as well as goods.

Reflection Questions

1. How would blockchain-based authenticity records change the way you view luxury purchases?

2. Would proof of ethical sourcing influence your decision to buy from certain brands over others?

3. How might verified provenance impact the resale value of luxury items in your life?

4. What opportunities exist for smaller luxury brands to adopt blockchain without losing their unique heritage?

5. Could blockchain verification become such a standard that transparency itself becomes the baseline expectation for all purchases, not just luxury?

TRANSPARENCY IN LUXURY

- **COMBAT COUNTERFEITING**
- **VERIFY AUTHENTICITY**
- **BUILD TRUST**

CHAPTER 26

How Blockchain Is Democratizing Access to Capital

By removing middlemen and lowering barriers, blockchain is making it possible for more people to invest, fundraise, and grow wealth.

Technology changes who gets access. For most of modern finance, access to capital depended on location, gatekeepers, and legacy rules. Entrepreneurs pitched a handful of firms on Sand Hill Road. Savers earned what their bank offered. Ordinary investors waited for institutions to move first. That world is shifting. Blockchain lowers the friction to create, move, and prove ownership of value, which is unlocking new paths to raise funds, lend, borrow, and invest at a global scale.

This chapter looks at capital markets as a whole and focuses on areas that extend well beyond real estate. You will see how founders reach backers across borders, how individuals can lend or borrow without a bank, how communities pool resources for shared goals, how entirely new asset classes are opening to broader participation, and how large institutions are building the rails for mainstream adoption. You will also see the risks and the rules taking shape.

Startup fundraising and venture capital, reimagined

Raising money used to mean cold introductions and a narrow circle of investors. Blockchain allows founders to create compliant digital representations of equity or revenue rights, then place them in front of a global pool of accredited participants or, in some jurisdictions, qualified retail backers through regulated crowdfunding. Smart contracts automate tasks that once required teams of lawyers and transfer agents, such as cap table updates, vesting logic, and dividend or revenue sharing.

A typical journey now looks like this. A company forms, sets its governance and disclosure terms, and issues a limited series of digital securities through a licensed platform. Investors complete identity checks, review standardized documents, and subscribe from anywhere the offering is permitted. Settlement is near instant. Holders can receive on-chain distributions when revenue hits a predetermined threshold. Secondary trading can occur on regulated alternative trading systems that list compliant digital securities, which increases optionality for early investors and employees.

Prominent institutions such as BlackRock, Franklin Templeton, and Goldman Sachs have already issued tokenized funds and bonds, while KKR and Hamilton Lane have tokenized private equity funds to reach a broader base of investors. The practical impact is reach and speed. Founders can test market demand early and more transparently. Niche ventures can aggregate supporters who believe in the thesis even if they live far from traditional hubs. Investor relations become data driven because on-chain ownership and engagement can be measured with precision.

Beyond securities: alternative fundraising models

Not every blockchain-based raise has to involve issuing securities. Founders have other ethical, legal ways to engage backers and bring in early capital, especially when the goal is access, utility, or pre-purchased services rather than ownership or profit rights.

Utility tokens grant holders the ability to use a product or network. A decentralized storage project, for example, can sell tokens that redeem for storage space. Buyers become early users rather than investors, and the token represents prepaid access to a service.

Membership passes or NFTs can provide digital entry points. A startup can issue NFTs that serve as club memberships, event tickets, or subscription credentials. The value lies in what the pass unlocks, not in speculative returns. Global brands like Nike, Adidas, and Starbucks have used blockchain-based passes to grant members access to exclusive drops, events, and loyalty programs.

Product pre-sales on chain mirror familiar crowdfunding models but add transparency and global reach. A company can sell digital vouchers for the first production run of a new device, creating upfront capital while promising delivery of goods rather than equity.

Revenue-sharing agreements can also be tokenized. In some cases, holders receive a portion of future revenue from a specific project or line of business without owning stock in the company. These arrangements must be structured carefully, since they approach the line of what regulators may consider a security.

Programmable flows are also emerging as another path. Smart contracts can distribute income or rewards in real time, using stablecoins to recognize contributions without conferring ownership stakes.

The key is that these models must avoid promising profit from "the efforts of others," which is the central standard regulators use under the Howey Test in the United States. When structured as access, prepayment, or participation, these tools open capital formation while staying aligned with both ethics and compliance.

DeFi lending and borrowing, credit without a branch

Decentralized finance protocols match lenders and borrowers through transparent rules that anyone can inspect. Individuals deposit assets into shared liquidity pools and earn a programmatic yield. Borrowers post collateral or supply verifiable real-world receivables to draw credit lines. Interest rates adjust in real time based on supply and demand.

Liquidations are automated when collateral ratios fall, which reduces manual intervention and hidden delays.

There are two broad models. Overcollateralized markets support quick access to credit for traders and developers who need working capital. Underwriting is algorithmic and backed by assets that the protocol can value and liquidate. The second model connects on-chain liquidity to off-chain borrowers. Service providers originate small business loans, revenue share agreements, or short-dated invoices, then tokenize them and place them into permissioned pools for qualified lenders. This bridges the savings of individuals with the capital needs of real companies.

Aave, Compound, and MakerDAO are the most widely used protocols, with billions in active liquidity. At the same time, companies like Goldfinch and Maple Finance connect decentralized capital to real-world small business lending and credit markets. For savers in countries with limited deposit products, these platforms can provide yields that are visible and auditable in real time. For small businesses, they can shorten the time from application to funding and open doors that were previously closed by geography.

Community driven financing, a brief look

Communities can organize capital around a clear mission. Members contribute funds into a shared treasury, vote on allocations, and track every disbursement on chain. Research groups fund open science, local groups back neighborhood projects, and collectors pool resources to acquire cultural assets. Shared treasuries plus transparent rules enable collective capital formation at internet speed. Gitcoin, for example, has distributed over $60 million to open-source projects using community-driven funding rounds.

New asset classes, from creative rights to climate markets

Once value can be defined and verified in software, new investable categories emerge.

Music royalties can be split into digital shares that entitle holders to a portion of future streaming revenue. Artists can raise funds directly from fans and share upside as success accrues. Royal.io and AnotherBlock have pioneered this model by tokenizing shares of songs from mainstream artists like The Chainsmokers and Justin Bieber's catalog.

Carbon credits and environmental assets benefit from auditable tracking. Registry-linked tokens can reduce double counting and make provenance clear. Programmable rules can retire credits automatically once a claim is made, which strengthens integrity. Organizations such as The World Bank, and the United Nations Climate Change Secretariat (UNFCCC) are advancing blockchain-based carbon markets, while companies like Shell are testing blockchain for transparent carbon reporting.

Sports and fandom are evolving into participatory economies. Teams and leagues can create compliant digital instruments that give supporters access to verified experiences, voting on club matters that are appropriate for fans, or a share of commercial revenue where regulations allow. FIFA, through its partnership with Algorand, and NBA Top Shot, created by Dapper Labs, are high-profile examples that show how global sports leagues are using blockchain to engage fans.

Intellectual property can be financed in new ways. Patents, research rights, and trademarks can be packaged into revenue-sharing vehicles. Backers fund development and receive distributions tied to licensing income. This helps scientists and creators tap global capital without leaving ownership entirely in the hands of a single firm. IPwe, a blockchain-based patent platform, is working with major corporations to tokenize patent portfolios for broader financing and licensing.

Financial inclusion, access as a design goal

Billions of people live with limited access to affordable credit and high-quality savings. Blockchain-based rails are lowering those barriers in measurable ways.

Remittances can settle in minutes at a fraction of traditional costs. A worker can send value home using a regulated wallet and a well-known stablecoin, then the recipient can cash out locally or spend directly with a merchant who accepts digital payments. Because settlement is final and visible, both sides gain confidence. Stellar and MoneyGram have partnered to power remittance corridors worldwide, bringing blockchain access to millions.

Savings can earn a yield even when local banks offer little. A villager with a smartphone can place a small amount into a transparent pool and watch interest accrue block by block. With responsible onboarding and education, these tools become a bridge to financial stability rather than a source of risk.

New services like Astra are designing programmable flows so income can be allocated the instant it arrives. Through smart contract automation, a paycheck can be divided across savings, bills, investments, and spending accounts without delay. Every dollar can begin earning interest the moment it arrives, flowing into savings, investments, or yield-generating accounts, while still remaining accessible whenever needed.

Platforms like Zebec take the idea further with real-time payroll streaming. Instead of waiting two weeks, employees can receive compensation continuously, down to the second, in stablecoins. Companies gain efficiency and compliance, while workers gain liquidity and confidence. These models show how access to capital is shifting from periodic disbursements to continuous flow, broadening inclusion, and reshaping the worker-employer relationship.

Micro and small enterprises can present tokenized invoices or point-of-sale revenue streams to global lenders. Underwriting data can be signed by verified devices or payment processors, which reduces fraud and speeds decisions. Capital flows toward productive uses rather than being trapped by distance.

Institutional adoption, building the rails at scale

Large asset managers, banks, and market utilities are not watching from the sidelines. They are piloting tokenized money market funds, sovereign and corporate bonds, and collateral management systems on permissioned and public chains.

BlackRock, the world's largest asset manager, launched its first tokenized money market fund in 2023, settling transactions on Ethereum. Franklin Templeton and

WisdomTree have also issued tokenized funds, with assets recorded directly on blockchain. Banks such as JPMorgan, through its Onyx platform, are testing delivery-versus-payment with atomic settlement across currencies and securities.

Market infrastructures are building gateways so that on-chain ownership can interoperate with existing clearing and settlement. The Depository Trust & Clearing Corporation (DTCC) in the U.S. and the Singapore Exchange (SGX) have both run tokenization pilots. Sovereign wealth funds and public pension plans are engaging through sandboxes and consortiums that focus on tokenized treasuries, repo, and private market funds. The appeal is operational efficiency, real-time transparency, and the ability to serve global participants with lower friction. The direction of travel is clear. Core parts of capital markets are being rebuilt with programmable money, programmable assets, and programmable rules.

Risks and the regulatory landscape

Democratizing access is meaningful only if it is safe. That requires thoughtful guardrails.

Compliance frameworks are evolving. Jurisdictions are clarifying how digital assets fit within existing securities, payments, and commodities laws. Licensed platforms are implementing identity checks, disclosures, and market surveillance. Stablecoin issuers are adopting stronger reserve standards and attestations. Custody standards are maturing with qualified custodians and segregation of client assets.

Investor protection is central. Code must be audited. Oracles and data feeds must be resilient. Protocols must publish risk metrics that users can understand. Offerings must provide clear information on what holders own and how they can exit.

Governments are experimenting with policy sandboxes so innovation can proceed under supervision. Central banks are testing wholesale settlement on distributed ledgers. Financial stability authorities are monitoring leverage and interconnectedness to reduce systemic risk. Builders and policymakers are learning together, which is the only way to make the transition durable.

What this means for founders, savers, and institutions

For founders, the fundraising map is wider. You can reach supporters in multiple regions, tailor instruments to your business model, and manage ownership with software. The burden is to disclose clearly, comply with the rules where you operate, and choose partners who value long-term trust.

For savers and individual investors, opportunity expands, but so does responsibility. Diversification, careful platform selection, and an understanding of how returns are generated are essential. The benefit is transparency you can verify yourself rather than taking it on faith. Emerging platforms like Astra and Zebec highlight the need to evaluate new models carefully, but they also demonstrate how quickly personal finance is evolving toward programmable money.

For institutions, the choice is to lead the transition or adapt to it. Tokenized models are not a side project. They are becoming the operating system for issuance, trading, collateral, and reporting. The firms that standardize workflows and educate clients now will set the benchmarks others follow.

A closing perspective

Access to capital shapes what gets built. When access is concentrated, ideas wait for permission. When access opens, more people build, more people invest, and more value circulates where it is needed. Blockchain is not a shortcut. It is infrastructure that lowers friction, widens participation, and makes commitments verifiable. That is how markets grow more inclusive without losing rigor.

Key Takeaways

• BlackRock, Franklin Templeton, and Goldman Sachs are leading the way in tokenized securities and funds
• Global brands like Nike and Starbucks are using blockchain for memberships and loyalty that double as fundraising models
• DeFi platforms such as Aave and MakerDAO are redefining lending and borrowing at global scale
• Verra, World Bank, and Shell are applying blockchain to carbon markets and sustainability tracking
• FIFA's Algorand partnership and NBA Top Shot show how sports and entertainment are opening new asset classes

---

Reflection Questions

1. How could tokenized funds from BlackRock or Goldman Sachs change access to capital in your field?

2. What insights can be drawn from Nike and Starbucks using blockchain passes that might inspire your business model?

3. Could DeFi lending through platforms like Aave or MakerDAO expand financial opportunity where you live or work?

4. How might blockchain-powered carbon tracking from Verra or the World Bank influence your sustainability strategies?

5. What opportunities exist for engaging your community through blockchain the way FIFA and the NBA are engaging fans?

Chapter 27

Blockchain and the Built World: Architecture, Cities, and Supply Chains

Explore how blockchain is influencing infrastructure, from smart cities to construction timelines and sustainable sourcing.

The systems that create and sustain our physical world are some of the most complex on Earth. Roads, bridges, buildings, and supply chains involve thousands of moving parts, each with stakeholders, contracts, and resources that must align for the project to succeed. Historically, this sector has been plagued by inefficiencies, delays, opaque practices, and waste. Now blockchain is stepping in as a technology capable of bringing transparency, accountability, and efficiency into the built world.

From how skyscrapers are constructed, to how cities monitor their infrastructure, to how raw materials are sourced across continents, blockchain is beginning to play a decisive role. It offers a way to track every stage of the process, verify authenticity, enforce agreements, and connect information across multiple organizations that often do not fully trust each other. As infrastructure spending surges worldwide and smart city initiatives accelerate, blockchain is no longer an experiment on the sidelines. It is becoming an essential tool for building and managing the environments we live and work in.

The Construction Industry: Building with Transparency

Construction projects are notorious for running over budget and behind schedule. The complexity of coordinating architects, engineers, contractors, subcontractors, and suppliers often creates silos of information where errors or fraud can hide. Studies have shown that large construction projects take 20 percent longer to finish than planned and can cost up to 80 percent more than their original budgets.

Blockchain can address these challenges by serving as a single source of truth across all stakeholders. Every contract, permit, payment, and inspection record can be anchored to a blockchain ledger. Smart contracts can automatically release funds when conditions are met, such as the verified completion of a building phase or the delivery of certified materials.

For example, firms in Europe and the Middle East are piloting blockchain-based systems where delivery receipts for cement, steel, and glass are logged in real time. These receipts are tied to Internet of Things (IoT) sensors that verify weight, quality, and delivery location. Once confirmed, smart contracts trigger payments to suppliers without delays or disputes. The result is reduced fraud, faster payment cycles, and greater accountability. In the United Arab Emirates, ALEC Engineering has tested blockchain to connect verified deliveries directly to automated payments, while in Europe, Arup has partnered with Concordium to explore blockchain for transparent materials tracking.

The approach is not limited to regional pilots. Skanska in Europe and Turner Construction in the United States have experimented with blockchain to streamline contract management and tie payment milestones directly to verified site activity. China State Construction Engineering Corporation (CSCEC), the largest builder in the world, has launched blockchain pilots to reduce fraud and inefficiencies in massive infrastructure projects. Startups such as Brickschain are pushing this further by creating project management platforms that extend blockchain transparency across entire construction lifecycles. The impact goes beyond efficiency: transparency reduces opportunities for corruption, a problem that costs the global construction sector billions annually.

Architecture and Design: From Vision to Verified Execution

Architects operate in a world of creativity and compliance. Designs must balance aesthetic ambition with safety regulations, zoning requirements, and sustainability goals. Often, architectural plans go through dozens of revisions as they move from digital blueprints to physical construction. Miscommunication between architects, contractors, and regulators is one of the leading causes of cost overruns.

Blockchain allows every version of a design to be immutably recorded. Anchoring every version of a plan, permit, or material certification to a blockchain ledger, there's one shared truth accessible to all parties. This not only eliminates outdated documents but also cuts disputes, reduces fraud, ensures compliance, and shortens project timelines. Additionally, blockchain can store certifications for materials and design approvals, ensuring that the final building reflects the intended safety and environmental standards.

This process is being advanced in Singapore, recognized globally as a leader in smart building regulation. The Infocomm Media Development Authority (IMDA) has piloted blockchain platforms that automate permit approvals and link architectural designs directly to verified building codes. Developers such as CapitaLand, one of

Asia's largest real estate groups, are also exploring blockchain to connect compliance with sustainability certifications. By embedding approvals and standards on-chain, Singapore is showing how design-to-build timelines can be shortened dramatically while reducing errors and compliance risks.

Smart Cities: Blockchain as the Nervous System

Cities are ecosystems of infrastructure, data, and people. As urban populations grow, expected to reach nearly 70 percent of the world's population by 2050, the need for efficient, secure, and transparent city management is urgent. Smart city initiatives aim to integrate digital technologies into urban environments, from traffic lights that adapt to congestion to energy grids that balance demand in real time. Blockchain is emerging as the backbone of these projects by providing secure and interoperable data exchange across multiple systems.

Dubai has become the world's most ambitious example of blockchain at the citywide level. Its Smart Dubai initiative has launched dozens of blockchain pilots across government services, property transactions, and energy management. The city's land department records real estate ownership on blockchain to reduce fraud, while utilities have introduced blockchain-enabled peer-to-peer solar energy trading. By 2030, Dubai aims to be the first city fully powered by blockchain-based public services, positioning itself as the benchmark for large-scale adoption.

Other cities are following with their own focus areas. Seoul has piloted blockchain for citizen services, including voting and welfare distribution. In China, cities such as Hangzhou and Shenzhen are developing blockchain identity platforms to simplify access to healthcare, transportation, and government programs. Within the European Union, the European Blockchain Services Infrastructure (EBSI) integrates blockchain into municipal sustainability planning, allowing verified data on emissions and energy use to be shared across borders. Utilities are also experimenting, from Power Ledger in Australia, which enables neighborhoods to trade excess solar energy, to the Brooklyn Microgrid in New York, which showed how communities can settle local energy trades without relying on a central authority.

For cities, blockchain is becoming more than a digital layer. In Dubai it is the foundation for citywide governance, while in regions like Singapore and the EU it strengthens specific systems such as compliance and sustainability. Together, these models illustrate how blockchain is evolving into the nervous system that connects diverse infrastructures securely and transparently.

Supply Chains: From Raw Materials to Finished Structures

Every piece of infrastructure, from a steel beam in a bridge to a pane of glass in a skyscraper, passes through supply chains before arriving on site. These construction supply chains are vast, often opaque, and vulnerable to inefficiency, counterfeiting, and unethical sourcing. Blockchain provides a way to verify every step of the journey, creating a transparent chain of custody that anyone can audit.

Steel can now be traced back to its origin, with blockchain records documenting the mine it came from, the methods of production, the environmental footprint, and every transfer point until delivery. This assures quality while addressing rising demands for sustainable and ethical sourcing. Holcim, one of the world's largest cement producers, has tested blockchain to track emissions and recycled inputs across its supply chain, while ArcelorMittal has explored blockchain to certify sustainable steel production.

Timber is another critical material for construction. In 2024, major suppliers in Asia began certifying provenance on blockchain to guarantee that wood comes from legal and sustainable forests. This helps developers align with international environmental standards and meet green building certifications. Acciona, a global leader in sustainable infrastructure, has piloted blockchain to verify renewable materials in its construction projects.

Luxury developers are also adopting blockchain to verify sourcing of rare materials such as marble and exotic woods. Everledger and De Beers, already known for applying blockchain to diamonds and gemstones, are extending these systems to high-value architectural inputs, ensuring they are ethically and sustainably sourced before being used in landmark projects.

Sustainability and the Green Transition

The built world is one of the largest contributors to global carbon emissions. Construction, building operations, and material sourcing together account for nearly 40 percent of annual greenhouse gas emissions. Achieving global climate goals requires rethinking how buildings are designed, constructed, and managed throughout their life cycles. Blockchain plays a growing role in that transition.

By tracking emissions data across supply chains and construction phases, blockchain creates verifiable sustainability records. These records can be tied to green financing, carbon credits, and regulatory compliance. Investors increasingly demand transparent environmental reporting, and blockchain makes it possible to verify that claims of sustainable construction are accurate.

In Europe, real estate firms are issuing blockchain-based sustainability certificates tied to properties, verifying energy efficiency, material sourcing, and operational performance. The Energy Web Foundation integrates blockchain into renewable energy tracking, allowing buildings and cities to prove their energy comes from verified clean sources.

By aligning construction with the UN's Sustainable Development Goals, blockchain ensures accountability across all participants.

Global Leaders and Corporate Adoption

Beyond pilots, blockchain is being adopted at scale in infrastructure and supply chain projects worldwide.

- **IBM** has adapted its blockchain models for construction logistics and infrastructure.
- **Siemens** explores blockchain for energy efficient building management, linking smart meters and decentralized grids.
- **Acciona**, a global leader in sustainable infrastructure, uses blockchain to certify renewable energy usage.
- **Trimble**, a construction technology giant, integrates blockchain into project management platforms.
- **CSCEC**, the largest construction company in the world, has launched blockchain pilots for supply chain management.
- **World Bank** pioneered blockchain bonds to fund infrastructure and continues to issue digital debt securities.
- **European Investment Bank (EIB)** issued a €100 million bond on Ethereum, showing institutional confidence in blockchain financing.

These examples confirm that blockchain is being integrated into some of the world's largest construction, infrastructure, and financing projects.

The Human Dimension: Why This Matters

The built world is not only about materials and logistics; it is about people. Cities, buildings, and infrastructure form the environments where billions of people live, work, and dream. Blockchain's integration into these systems is not about replacing human expertise but about enhancing trust, efficiency, and resilience.

For citizens, blockchain-enabled infrastructure means safer buildings, more reliable services, and sustainable environments. For governments, it provides accountability in public spending and ensures that projects are delivered as promised. For businesses, it opens new efficiencies, reduces risk, and creates verifiable value.

As climate pressures mount and urbanization accelerates, the need for systems that are transparent, accountable, and adaptable has never been greater. Blockchain, combined with other digital technologies, is laying the foundation for a future where the built environment reflects not only human creativity but also human responsibility.

Key Takeaways

• Blockchain is improving construction efficiency with transparent records, smart contracts, and pilots by firms such as Skanska, Turner Construction, and CSCEC

• Architectural plans and approvals are being anchored to blockchain in regions like Singapore, reducing errors and delays

• Smart cities from Dubai to Seoul to the EU's EBSI initiative are embedding blockchain in governance, property, and utilities

• Supply chains are becoming more transparent through IBM, Maersk, Walmart, De Beers, and Everledger verifying provenance and sustainability

• Global corporations and institutions like Siemens, Acciona, Holcim, World Bank, and EIB are scaling blockchain adoption across infrastructure and energy

---

Reflection Questions

1. How could blockchain reduce inefficiencies or fraud in the construction and infrastructure projects you encounter?

2. What benefits would transparent, blockchain-based supply chains bring to industries you interact with?

3. In what ways could blockchain-enabled smart city services improve your daily life or your community's quality of living?

4. How might blockchain-based sustainability records influence your decisions as a consumer, investor, or citizen?

5. What opportunities exist for your organization to lead in integrating blockchain into the built world?

Chapter 28

Global Supply Chains

How blockchain is transforming the way goods move around the world, from verifying raw materials and securing shipping documentation to ensuring ethical sourcing and streamlining global trade.

Supply chains are the invisible networks that keep the modern world running. From the food in supermarkets to the smartphones in our pockets, every product depends on complex, global pathways of materials, manufacturing, transport, and trade. Yet these systems are often opaque and fragile. Counterfeit goods slip into markets, delays pile up at ports, and consumers are left with little insight into where their products come from or how they were made.

Blockchain is reshaping this landscape by making supply chains transparent, auditable, and verifiable at every stage. By anchoring transactions and certifications on-chain, companies and governments gain shared visibility into the journey of goods. For industries, this reduces fraud, errors, and delays. For consumers, it builds trust in the products they buy. And for the planet, it creates accountability around sustainability and ethical sourcing.

Traceability from Origin to Shelf

One of blockchain's most significant contributions to supply chains is traceability. For decades, companies relied on paper records, siloed databases, or manual declarations to track materials. These methods are slow, prone to errors, and easily manipulated. Blockchain introduces a tamper-proof record of origin and custody.

Food safety has been a leading driver. Walmart, Carrefour, and Nestlé have used IBM Food Trust to trace items like lettuce, mangoes, and baby food. What once took days of paperwork to verify can now be confirmed in seconds by scanning a QR code linked to blockchain records. This not only protects consumers but also helps companies react instantly to contamination incidents, isolating affected products and preventing recalls from spiraling.

Pharmaceuticals are another sector where traceability is critical. Counterfeit drugs cost the industry billions annually and threaten lives. The U.S. Food and Drug Administration's Drug Supply Chain Security Act has prompted companies like Pfizer and Moderna to test blockchain to verify every step from manufacturing to pharmacy. By logging serial numbers and shipping events immutably, blockchain ensures that medicines are authentic and safely handled.

Mining and natural resources are also embracing traceability. BHP has piloted blockchain to track ore samples across global supply routes, ensuring quality and compliance with safety regulations. Similarly, De Beers' Tracr platform verifies that diamonds are ethically sourced and free from conflict. By extending blockchain into rare earth minerals and metals like cobalt, companies are addressing the demand for ethically sourced materials in electronics and electric vehicles.

Shipping and Logistics

Global trade moves at the scale of trillions of dollars annually, yet much of the system still depends on paper bills of lading and manual customs processes. Blockchain is modernizing these systems.

Maersk and IBM launched TradeLens, a platform that digitized shipping documentation. At its peak, TradeLens connected over 300 organizations, including ports, customs agencies, and shipping lines. Although Maersk wound down the platform in 2023 due to adoption challenges, the experiment proved blockchain's potential for faster, more transparent trade flows. Building on that foundation, other logistics providers and governments are now adapting similar solutions to streamline customs and reduce bottlenecks.

DHL and FedEx have tested blockchain to verify international shipping data, reducing disputes and ensuring parcels meet regulatory requirements. In ports across Europe and Asia, customs authorities are piloting blockchain systems to share container data instantly across jurisdictions, cutting clearance times from days to hours.

Even in air cargo, blockchain is gaining ground. The International Air Transport Association (IATA) has explored blockchain for digital waybills, helping airlines and shippers eliminate redundant paperwork. The ability to share a single version of truth across multiple carriers improves efficiency while reducing fraud in high-value shipments.

Ethical and Sustainable Sourcing

Modern consumers demand more than speed and price. They want to know whether their products are ethically made and environmentally responsible. Blockchain provides the transparency needed to back those claims with verifiable data.

In fashion, LVMH, Prada, and Cartier co-founded the Aura Blockchain Consortium to certify authenticity and sustainability of luxury goods. A handbag, watch, or pair of shoes can now be tied to a blockchain certificate that proves its origin, materials, and production process. For brands, this strengthens reputation and reduces counterfeiting. For consumers, it builds trust in the story behind what they purchase.

In timber and forestry, blockchain is addressing deforestation and illegal logging. Suppliers in Asia and South America are using blockchain records to certify that wood comes from legal and sustainable sources. Developers in Europe are adopting these systems to meet strict environmental standards and green building codes.

Energy and commodities are also part of this shift. The Energy Web Foundation has worked with utilities to track renewable energy credits, allowing companies to prove their power comes from verified clean sources.

Financing and Trade Flows

Beyond tracking goods, blockchain is transforming how supply chains are financed. Traditional trade finance relies on letters of credit, often involving multiple banks and weeks of processing. By digitizing these instruments on blockchain, settlement times drop dramatically.

The World Bank and the European Investment Bank (EIB) have both issued blockchain-based bonds to fund infrastructure and trade, signaling confidence in digital finance models. Private banks are following. HSBC and Standard Chartered have piloted blockchain for cross-border trade settlement, reducing costs and unlocking capital for businesses faster.

Small and medium-sized enterprises, often excluded from global trade finance, stand to benefit most. By tokenizing invoices and receivables, businesses can secure credit against verifiable on-chain records. This reduces risk for lenders and expands access to liquidity for smaller suppliers.

Resilience in a Fragile World

The COVID-19 pandemic exposed the fragility of global supply chains. Shortages of medical equipment, semiconductors, and food revealed how little visibility companies had into their own networks. Blockchain offers a path toward resilience by making supply chains transparent and adaptable.

Governments are now prioritizing digital infrastructure for supply chains. The U.S. Department of Homeland Security has funded blockchain pilots for critical supply chain security. The European Union's EBSI initiative is integrating blockchain into cross-border logistics. In Asia, countries like Singapore and South Korea are using blockchain to strengthen food, medical, and energy supply resilience.

For businesses, resilience means being able to see upstream risks earlier, verify suppliers instantly, and adapt financing dynamically. Blockchain creates the trusted data foundation needed to support that adaptability.

The Human Dimension: Why This Matters

Supply chains might seem like technical back-office processes, but they touch every aspect of human life. When food recalls are faster, lives are saved. When medicines are verified, patients gain safety. When timber, minerals, and energy are traced, consumers can buy with confidence that their purchases align with their values.

For businesses, blockchain-enabled supply chains create efficiency, reduce fraud, and open access to financing. For governments, they provide tools to secure national infrastructure and reduce systemic risk. For the planet, they create accountability in how resources are extracted, traded, and consumed.

Supply chains are the arteries of the global economy. By bringing transparency and trust into these arteries, blockchain is not only making trade more efficient but also more ethical and resilient.

Key Takeaways

• Blockchain enhances traceability across supply chains, verifying origin and custody of goods from food to pharmaceuticals to raw materials

• Global logistics providers like DHL, FedEx, and IATA are adopting blockchain to digitize documentation and reduce bottlenecks

• Luxury and consumer brands are using blockchain to certify authenticity and sustainability, from fashion to timber to clean energy

• Financial institutions and development banks are piloting blockchain-based trade finance, unlocking faster settlement and wider access to liquidity

• Governments and corporations are embedding blockchain into supply chain security and resilience strategies worldwide

---

Reflection Questions

1. Where in your industry could blockchain-enabled traceability improve trust in products or services?

2. How might blockchain-based trade finance expand opportunities for smaller suppliers or entrepreneurs you work with?

3. What risks in your supply chain would be reduced if every step were verified on blockchain?

4. In what ways could blockchain transparency strengthen sustainability and ethical sourcing in areas you care about?

5. How could blockchain-enabled resilience prepare your community or organization for future global disruptions?

Chapter 29

Unlocking Global Participation: Empowering the Unbanked

Billions of people excluded from traditional banking systems are gaining access to tools for earning, saving, and building wealth.

Billions of people excluded from traditional banking systems are gaining access to tools for earning, saving, and building wealth.

Financial exclusion is one of the most persistent barriers to global prosperity. According to the World Bank, more than 1.4 billion adults remain unbanked, about 24 percent of the world's adults, roughly 1 in 4 people over age the age of 15 globally. Meaning they do not have access to a formal savings account, credit, or the ability to securely send and receive money. Most of these individuals live in developing regions, where banking infrastructure is limited, documentation requirements are strict, and fees make services unaffordable for low-income populations.

The consequences are profound. Without access to banking, people cannot easily save for emergencies, borrow to grow businesses, or send money across borders. Women and rural populations are disproportionately excluded, limiting economic independence and participation. Financial exclusion locks individuals and entire communities out of the opportunities that create stability and growth.

Blockchain is changing this reality by lowering entry barriers and delivering financial services through mobile phones and digital networks. For the first time, people without access to traditional institutions can earn, save, and transact securely, often with just a smartphone and internet connection. The technology is providing the infrastructure for financial participation at a global scale, where inclusion is not a privilege but a baseline.

Mobile Money and Digital Wallets

The rise of mobile money has already proven that access does not require traditional banks. In Kenya, M-Pesa revolutionized financial access by allowing people to send and receive funds through simple text messages. More than 50 million users now rely on M-Pesa across Africa, and studies show that it has lifted hundreds of thousands out of poverty by enabling small business creation and secure household savings.

Blockchain-based wallets build on this model, offering global access, lower transaction costs, and additional features like savings, credit, and insurance. Platforms such as Stellar have partnered with financial institutions to provide cross-border remittance services, connecting local mobile money networks to blockchain rails. Ripple's XRP-based payment solutions are being used by providers in the Philippines, Mexico, and Africa to reduce the cost of sending money home, making remittances faster and more affordable for millions of migrant workers.

Unlike traditional mobile money that often operates within a single country, blockchain-enabled wallets are borderless. A person in Uganda can receive stablecoins from a family member in London in minutes, with fees far lower than traditional remittance providers. That same wallet can also hold tokenized savings, connect to local merchants, and build a digital transaction history that can serve as a credit record.

Identity and Access

One of the greatest challenges in reaching the unbanked is the lack of formal identification. The World Bank estimates that nearly 850 million people globally lack official identity documents, making it impossible to open accounts, register businesses, or access government services.

Blockchain is being applied to create decentralized digital identities that do not depend on fragile or exclusionary state systems. In India, the Aadhaar program has issued digital IDs linked to biometric data, connecting hundreds of millions to financial and government services. While Aadhaar itself is not blockchain-based, similar approaches are now being built on decentralized ledgers to ensure privacy, portability, and verifiability.

Projects like ID2020 and initiatives led by the World Food Programme use blockchain to provide refugees and displaced persons with digital identities that allow them to receive aid, access banking, and rebuild their lives even without formal paperwork. In regions where statelessness or migration prevent access to traditional services, blockchain-based identity becomes the gateway to participation.

Savings and Microfinance

For unbanked populations, the ability to save securely is often as important as borrowing. Without access to banks, many rely on cash, which is vulnerable to theft, inflation, and instability. Blockchain-based savings platforms enable individuals to hold assets in stablecoins, protecting their value against local currency volatility.

In Latin America, where inflation has eroded the value of local currencies, millions of people have turned to dollar-pegged stablecoins as a store of value. By using mobile apps, families can preserve their earnings without needing access to a bank branch. These tools turn savings into a possibility where traditional systems fail.

Microfinance institutions are also integrating blockchain to expand their reach. Organizations can issue loans directly to digital wallets, with repayment terms governed by smart contracts. The transparency of blockchain reduces fraud and lowers operational costs, allowing lenders to serve rural populations that were previously unreachable.

Remittances and Cross-Border Payments

Remittances are lifelines for many developing countries, often accounting for a significant portion of GDP. Yet traditional remittance services are expensive, with fees averaging 6 percent globally and higher in rural regions. Blockchain-based systems are reducing those costs dramatically.

Companies like Western Union and MoneyGram have piloted blockchain solutions to settle payments more efficiently. Startups using networks like Stellar and Ripple have already made it possible to send money across borders for a fraction of the cost, often settling in under a minute. For families depending on remittances for food, education, and healthcare, these savings translate into real impact.

In the Caribbean, the rise of central bank digital currencies (CBDCs) such as the Bahamian Sand Dollar shows how blockchain-backed solutions can extend financial inclusion. By combining regulated CBDCs with blockchain wallets, governments are creating systems that serve both domestic and cross-border needs at low cost.

Humanitarian Aid and Social Impact

Blockchain is also being applied to humanitarian aid, where inefficiency and lack of transparency have long undermined impact. The World Food Programme's Building Blocks initiative uses blockchain to deliver food and cash assistance directly to refugees in Jordan. By recording entitlements and purchases on blockchain, the program reduces fraud, speeds delivery, and gives recipients dignity in choosing their own meals.

Binance Charity has experimented with blockchain-based donations in Africa, ensuring that funds reach beneficiaries transparently and securely. In disaster relief scenarios, blockchain can provide instant disbursements that bypass corrupt intermediaries and deliver aid directly to those who need it most.

The Human Dimension: Stories of Impact

Behind every statistic are stories of people whose lives change with access. A farmer in rural Kenya using blockchain-based microloans to buy fertilizer and double his harvest. A domestic worker in Dubai sending stablecoins home to her family in the Philippines, who receive funds instantly instead of waiting days. A refugee in Jordan using a blockchain-based identity to purchase food with dignity in a camp store.

These stories illustrate that blockchain's promise for the unbanked is not about abstract technology. It is about giving people the tools to secure their futures, participate in economies, and build wealth that can be passed to the next generation. For me, this mission is deeply personal. Center for Creators was founded on the belief that every individual deserves the tools to grow, participate, and prosper, not as an exception, but as a standard of global inclusion.

The Path Forward

For blockchain to realize its full potential in financial inclusion, challenges remain. Education is essential to ensure new users understand both the benefits and risks. Mobile infrastructure must be extended to reach rural populations. Regulatory frameworks must balance innovation with consumer protection.

Yet the direction of travel is clear. Financial inclusion is no longer a side project for development agencies. It is becoming a global priority, with blockchain serving as one of the most powerful tools to bridge the gap. By empowering the unbanked, blockchain is not just transforming markets but reshaping what participation in the global economy means.

Key Takeaways

• More than 1.4 billion adults remain unbanked, but blockchain lowers barriers to savings, credit, and secure transactions
• Mobile money platforms like M-Pesa proved access can thrive without banks, and blockchain wallets expand this model globally
• Digital identity initiatives using blockchain give stateless and undocumented people access to services and participation
• Stablecoins and blockchain-based remittances reduce costs and settlement times, directly improving household stability
• Humanitarian aid programs use blockchain for transparency and dignity, ensuring assistance reaches those most in need

---

Reflection Questions

1. Where in your community or industry do you see people excluded from traditional financial systems?

2. How could blockchain-based wallets or remittance tools reduce costs or barriers for those populations?

3. What role might digital identity play in extending access to financial services globally?

4. How can your organization support financial literacy to help the unbanked adopt blockchain responsibly?

5. What partnerships could accelerate financial inclusion while ensuring transparency and trust?

Chapter 30

From Scarcity to Utility: The Shift from Speculation to Real Use Cases

The future of blockchain is about usefulness. This chapter explores how real-world utility is overtaking speculation.

The future of blockchain is about usefulness. Speculation may have captured the world's attention in the early days, but what will sustain this technology is how it solves real problems. Tokens, platforms, and networks are no longer measured only by scarcity or price charts. Their value is increasingly determined by whether they serve a purpose, create efficiencies, or unlock access to opportunities that did not exist before.

This shift marks blockchain's evolution from an experimental asset class into a foundational infrastructure. It is not about replacing money alone, but about weaving utility into industries as varied as healthcare, logistics, entertainment, identity, energy, and governance. The transition from scarcity to utility is how blockchain becomes not just known but indispensable.

The Speculative Era

The first decade of blockchain was defined by speculation. Bitcoin's rise introduced the idea that digital scarcity could hold value. Ethereum's launch brought programmable assets that multiplied possibilities. Alongside innovation, however, came a wave of tokens and projects that offered little more than promises.

The speculative period was not without value. It proved that global communities could form around code, that markets could respond to decentralized networks, and that scarcity alone could attract capital. Yet speculation alone was never sustainable. Prices moved faster than adoption, and hype often overshadowed substance.

What followed was a necessary correction. Market downturns forced projects to demonstrate more than potential. Investors, regulators, and users began demanding proof of usefulness. That pressure is what has driven the next phase: the age of utility.

Defining Utility in Blockchain

Utility in blockchain is about solving real problems. A token or platform is useful if it improves how people transact, secure information, coordinate resources, or prove ownership. Scarcity may provide a foundation, but utility gives purpose.

Utility comes in many forms:

- Enabling cross-border transactions at lower cost and higher speed.
- Securing supply chains with tamper-proof records.
- Allowing creators to directly monetize their work.

- Bringing transparency to energy usage or carbon credits.

- Creating digital identities that unlock access to services.

Each of these represents not just a market opportunity but a structural improvement over the status quo. Utility is what moves blockchain from being an alternative to being essential.

Finance: Beyond Trading and Tokens

While speculation began in finance, it is also where some of the strongest real-world use cases have emerged. Stablecoins now settle billions of dollars in transactions every day, serving as rails for cross-border payments, payroll, and commerce. Companies like Visa and Mastercard are piloting blockchain settlement systems to move value instantly between institutions.

Capital markets are being restructured through tokenization. BlackRock and Fidelity are building platforms for tokenized funds and alternative investments. Governments and banks are testing blockchain for bond issuance, with the European Investment Bank pioneering digital bonds on public ledgers. These are not experiments on the sidelines; they are new standards forming at the center of finance.

Insurance firms are also exploring blockchain for claims management and risk pooling. Smart contracts automate payouts when pre-defined conditions are met, such as weather-based triggers for crop insurance. These innovations show that blockchain is not just about new currencies, but about making existing financial systems more efficient, transparent, and accessible.

Supply Chains and Logistics

Blockchain's ability to prove authenticity and track provenance is a powerful utility in supply chains. Companies like IBM, Maersk, and Walmart have already demonstrated how blockchain can reduce fraud, improve traceability, and speed up customs clearance.

Beyond pilots, industries are scaling adoption. Timber suppliers in Asia are certifying wood on blockchain to ensure legal and sustainable sourcing. The diamond industry, led by De Beers through its Tracr platform, tracks stones from mine to market to guarantee authenticity. Luxury goods conglomerates like LVMH use blockchain through the Aura consortium to give buyers digital certificates of authenticity, protecting brand value and consumer trust.

The utility here is clear. Counterfeiting, fraud, and inefficiency cost industries trillions annually. Blockchain reduces those losses and creates value by embedding trust into every link of the chain.

Healthcare and Identity

In healthcare, blockchain is being tested for secure medical record management. Patient data can be stored with privacy controls, accessible only to authorized providers, yet verifiable as complete and unaltered. Hospitals and research institutions in Europe and the United States are exploring blockchain to enable cross-border data sharing while preserving confidentiality.

Identity is another domain where blockchain's utility is transformative. Decentralized identity systems allow individuals to prove who they are without relying on fragile central registries. The European Union's EBSI initiative is advancing blockchain-based digital identities to allow citizens secure access to services across borders. For refugees and unbanked populations, blockchain identity becomes the key to accessing aid, opening accounts, or registering businesses.

This is utility that goes beyond efficiency. It is about enabling participation in fundamental systems of healthcare, commerce, and society.

Energy and Sustainability

The transition to renewable energy requires systems that are transparent, efficient, and adaptable. Blockchain is emerging as a backbone for this transition. Platforms like the Energy Web Foundation use blockchain to certify renewable energy production and consumption. This allows companies to prove their sustainability claims with tamper-proof records.

Peer-to-peer energy trading is another frontier. Power Ledger in Australia and projects in Europe have enabled households to sell excess solar energy directly to neighbors, recorded and settled on blockchain. This reduces waste, empowers consumers, and accelerates the adoption of clean energy.

Carbon markets are also being reshaped. By recording credits on blockchain, organizations like Verra are improving the integrity of carbon offsets, ensuring they are traceable and cannot be double counted. Utility here means aligning climate commitments with verifiable action.

Digital Ownership and Creative Economies

Creators have long faced barriers to monetizing their work, often surrendering revenue to intermediaries. Blockchain introduces new models for direct ownership and compensation.

In art and entertainment, platforms like Christie's and Sotheby's use blockchain for provenance tracking and digital auctions. Musicians can tokenize royalties, allowing fans to invest directly in their success. Writers and filmmakers are experimenting with blockchain-backed rights management to distribute revenue more fairly.

Gaming is another fast-growing sector of blockchain utility. Titles like Axie Infinity and The Sandbox have shown how blockchain enables players to own, trade, and monetize in-game assets. While not every experiment will endure, the model of digital ownership has become an irreversible shift in creative economies.

Government and Governance

Governments are adopting blockchain for functions that require transparency and trust. Land registries are being recorded on blockchain to reduce fraud and disputes, from **Georgia** to **Sweden**. Public procurement processes are being logged to ensure accountability.

Voting is another area of exploration. While challenges remain, pilots in countries such as Estonia and South Korea have tested blockchain for secure and transparent digital voting systems. If scaled responsibly, these systems could increase participation and trust in democratic processes.

The utility of governance applications is not about novelty. It is about embedding accountability where it matters most.

Why Utility Wins

Speculation may drive headlines, but utility is what drives adoption. The projects that endure will be those that serve real needs, integrate into existing systems, and create measurable value. In this phase, tokens are not judged by how scarce they are, but by how indispensable they become.

Utility is the bridge between blockchain's early promise and its long-term future. It is how technology moves from being interesting to being essential, from volatility to stability, from fringe to mainstream.

Key Takeaways

• The early era of blockchain was defined by speculation, but the future is about solving real problems

• Utility is emerging across finance, supply chains, healthcare, identity, energy, and creative industries

• Major corporations and governments are scaling blockchain use in payments, logistics, sustainability, and governance

• Tokens are increasingly valued for usefulness rather than scarcity, shifting blockchain into essential infrastructure

• Utility ensures blockchain's long-term role in global systems of commerce, identity, and trust

---

Reflection Questions

1. In your industry, where do you see blockchain moving from speculation to utility?

2. Which examples of blockchain adoption in finance, healthcare, or energy resonate most with your experience?

3. How might digital identity or ownership transform the way you or your organization operate?

4. What risks remain in focusing too heavily on speculation rather than long-term usefulness?

Chapter 31

What Comes After Hype: The Real-World Adoption of Blockchain Technology

As buzz fades, what remains is substance. Learn how blockchain is becoming the backbone of real systems in business, government, and life.

Every transformative technology passes through a cycle. First comes invention, then speculation, and then disillusionment as inflated expectations collide with reality. What follows is the quiet stage where substance emerges. Blockchain is moving through that stage now.

The headlines that once hyped prices, meme tokens, and overnight millionaires are fading. What remains are serious deployments by businesses, governments, and institutions that see blockchain as infrastructure, not novelty. This chapter looks at how real-world adoption is unfolding across sectors, where blockchain is proving essential, and why this phase matters more than any bull run or bubble that came before.

Moving Beyond the Hype Cycle

Technology research firms describe a curve where innovations peak in expectation, crash into disillusionment, and then climb toward productive adoption. Blockchain has traced that path. The speculative frenzy of 2017, the DeFi and NFT booms of 2020 and 2021, and the subsequent corrections shook out unsustainable projects. What is left are the builders and organizations embedding blockchain into systems that matter.

The significance of this stage is not quieter markets, but deeper integration. Real adoption means blockchain is being written into supply chain systems, payment rails, public registries, and corporate platforms. It is no longer about whether blockchain will survive, but about how it will scale.

Enterprise Adoption: From Pilot to Production

For years, enterprises experimented with blockchain in limited pilots. Today, some of the largest companies in the world are moving into production use.

- **IBM** has adapted its Food Trust model, used in retail, into logistics platforms for construction, pharmaceuticals, and critical supply chains.

- **Walmart** has expanded its blockchain use to track produce, pharmaceuticals, and imported goods, cutting investigation times from days to seconds.

- **Maersk** applied blockchain to global shipping documentation, proving that bills of lading could be digitized securely and efficiently. Even after winding down TradeLens in 2022 due to scaling challenges, the initiative set a benchmark for how shipping will evolve.

- **Siemens** is embedding blockchain into energy-efficient building systems and decentralized grids, treating it as an integral layer in its smart infrastructure portfolio.

- **JPMorgan** has deployed its Onyx blockchain platform to handle billions in daily transactions, from intraday repo settlements to cross-border payments, bringing blockchain into the heart of banking operations.

These examples highlight a key point: adoption is no longer limited to startups. It is being led by global incumbents that manage the backbone of trade, finance, and infrastructure.

Governments Stepping In

Public sector adoption is equally significant. Governments are discovering that blockchain provides transparency, efficiency, and accountability in areas that have historically been slow and opaque.

- **Dubai** has embedded blockchain across dozens of public services, including property registration, energy management, and healthcare licensing. Its ambition is to be the first city powered entirely by blockchain-enabled services.

- **United States** adoption has been more targeted yet impactful. The FDA's DSCSA pilot programs are testing blockchain for pharmaceutical traceability to ensure drug safety. At the state level, California's DMV has taken a major step by digitizing 42 million car titles on Avalanche's blockchain, enabling residents to claim their vehicle ownership via mobile wallets and reduce fraud significantly.

- **Estonia** uses blockchain to secure national registries, including health, property, and court systems, providing a model of digital governance for the world.

- **China** has piloted blockchain in judicial systems, supply chain finance, and citizen ID platforms. Courts accept blockchain-based evidence, and city governments in Hangzhou and Shenzhen are integrating it into administrative functions.

- **The European Union**, through its European Blockchain Services Infrastructure (EBSI), is standardizing blockchain-based public services across member states, including digital diplomas and sustainability tracking.

- **The World Bank and European Investment Bank** have both issued blockchain-based bonds, demonstrating that governments and supranational institutions trust blockchain for financing critical infrastructure.

Governments are not only legitimizing blockchain. They are institutionalizing it.

The Financial Sector: Integration at Scale

Banks once resisted blockchain, wary of disruption. Today, many are embracing it as a foundation for modernization.

- **BlackRock** and **Fidelity** have built tokenization platforms for funds and alternative assets, opening new access for investors.

- **BNY Mellon** now offers custody for digital assets alongside traditional securities, bridging old and new markets.

- **Visa** and **Mastercard** are trialing settlement networks that use stablecoins to move value instantly between banks and merchants.

- Central banks are piloting digital currencies for wholesale and retail settlement, with countries from Singapore to Sweden advancing projects that integrate blockchain-based rails into monetary policy.

The financial sector's adoption shows that blockchain is not parallel to the system. It is becoming part of the system itself.

Everyday Utility

Real-world adoption is not limited to governments and corporations. Individuals are already experiencing blockchain utility in ways that often go unnoticed.

- In Africa, platforms built on Stellar and Celo are providing wallets and remittance services for the unbanked.

- In Asia, ride-hailing apps are experimenting with blockchain-based loyalty rewards that can be exchanged across services.

- In Latin America, small businesses use blockchain platforms to access credit and protect themselves against inflation with stablecoins.

- In the United States and Europe, digital certificates of authenticity for luxury goods and art are quietly becoming standard, giving buyers confidence in provenance.

These are not speculative plays. They are everyday utilities where blockchain fades into the background but delivers real value.

Lessons from Failure

Adoption also comes with lessons. Not every blockchain project succeeds, even when backed by major institutions. Maersk's TradeLens ended because scaling global cooperation proved more difficult than technology itself. Many NFT platforms faded after speculative bubbles burst. Early experiments in decentralized autonomous organizations revealed governance weaknesses.

These failures are not signs of decline but of progress. They show where blockchain is useful and where it is not, helping the ecosystem refine its focus toward substance.

Why This Phase Matters

The post-hype phase is critical because it marks the transition from optional to essential. Blockchain is no longer waiting for validation. It has proven its worth in reducing fraud, cutting costs, improving transparency, and expanding access. The next challenge is scale: ensuring systems can handle billions of users, millions of transactions per second, and integration across borders and industries.

This is also the moment when leadership matters. The institutions and individuals who invest in education, infrastructure, and responsible regulation now will define how blockchain matures. Just as the internet became indispensable after its speculative bubble burst, blockchain is entering its defining stage of adoption.

Key Takeaways

• Blockchain has moved beyond hype into real-world adoption across business, government, and finance
• Enterprises like IBM, Walmart, Siemens, JPMorgan, and BNY Mellon are embedding blockchain into critical systems
• Governments from Dubai to Estonia to the European Union are institutionalizing blockchain in services and registries
• Financial institutions such as BlackRock, Fidelity, and central banks are integrating blockchain into mainstream finance
• Everyday adoption is visible in remittances, small business credit, and digital certificates of authenticity
• Failures like TradeLens show limits, but they also help refine blockchain's role and accelerate progress

---

Reflection Questions

1. In your field, where do you see blockchain moving from experiment to essential infrastructure?

2. Which examples of adoption by enterprises or governments feel most relevant to your experience?

3. How might failures and lessons from early blockchain projects inform future strategies?

4. What role should your organization or community play in supporting responsible adoption of blockchain?

5. How can you distinguish between projects that are still speculative and those proving real-world utility?

Chapter 32

How to Prepare for a Decentralized World

A practical exploration of how to adapt, participate, and thrive as power shifts from centralized control to distributed networks.

The shift toward decentralization is one of the defining transformations of our time. For centuries, individuals and organizations have relied on centralized authorities, including banks, governments, corporations, and institutions, to coordinate trust, validate ownership, and manage information. Blockchain has introduced an alternative: distributed networks where verification, exchange, and governance are shared among participants rather than controlled from the top down.

This shift is already visible in how we move money, verify identity, build communities, trade assets, and even design organizations. As decentralized models expand, the question becomes less about *whether* they will shape the future and more about *how to prepare*. For individuals, businesses, and governments, adapting to decentralization requires new mindsets, new tools, and new approaches to participation.

Understanding the Shift

At the core of decentralization is the transfer of trust. In centralized systems, trust resides in a single authority, whether it is a bank processing a payment or a government maintaining land titles. In decentralized systems, trust is established by code, consensus, and cryptography.

The implications are profound. Decentralization enables financial access for people excluded from banks. It allows creators to monetize their work directly with audiences. It enables communities to fund and govern projects without a central sponsor. It also introduces new forms of accountability since records on blockchain are transparent and tamper resistant.

Preparing for a decentralized world means recognizing that these changes are not confined to finance or technology. They affect how we live, work, and collaborate. The same way the internet redefined communication, decentralization is redefining trust and value.

Personal Preparation: Skills and Mindsets

For individuals, thriving in a decentralized world begins with developing new literacy. Financial literacy must now include digital wallets, stablecoins, and smart contracts. Professional literacy must extend to understanding how decentralized systems are reshaping industries. Civic literacy must include how governance and participation are being reimagined.

Practical steps include:

Learning to use digital wallets

Digital wallets are the starting point for almost every interaction on blockchain. Tools like MetaMask, Xaman, and Coinbase Wallet function as gateways to decentralized finance, digital identity, and applications. Just as learning to use email became essential in the 1990s, wallet literacy is quickly becoming foundational for participating in today's digital economy.

For beginners, MetaMask is one of the most widely used wallets. It connects easily to Ethereum and other compatible blockchains, allowing users to hold tokens, interact with applications, and even customize networks. Installing MetaMask, creating a recovery phrase, and practicing a simple transaction teaches essential habits of self-custody and security.

Xaman is purpose-built for the XRP Ledger and introduces beginners to features unique to this ecosystem. Unlike other networks, XRP accounts require a small reserve of XRP to activate, so setting up a Xaman wallet usually begins with transferring funds from an exchange like Coinbase. From there, beginners can add trustlines, view issued tokens, and experience how the XRP Ledger emphasizes security and permissioned access. This step highlights the importance of understanding how different blockchains handle ownership and participation.

Coinbase Wallet offers a more guided experience. It connects directly with Coinbase's exchange but operates as a self-custodial wallet, giving beginners full control of their assets. In addition to storing tokens, it allows users to explore NFTs, access decentralized exchanges, and try out Web3 applications in a secure environment that is familiar to many already using Coinbase for trading.

Across all of these options, the process of downloading, activating, and using a wallet helps beginners understand the foundations of blockchain: how value is stored, how identity is tied to keys rather than usernames, and how access to applications is secured. Mastering wallets is the first step toward mastering participation in a decentralized world.

Experimenting with decentralized applications

One of the simplest ways to understand blockchain is to interact with applications directly. With MetaMask, beginners can connect to decentralized finance platforms like Uniswap, where even a small token swap demonstrates how smart contracts execute transactions without a bank or broker. For those curious about blockchain beyond finance, Coinbase Wallet makes it easy to explore NFTs on marketplaces like OpenSea, showing how digital art and collectibles are owned and transferred transparently. Coinbase Wallet also opens access to decentralized exchanges, Web3 apps, and staking features, making it a versatile starting point for beginners who want to experience more than just token storage.

On the XRP Ledger, the Xaman Wallet lets beginners add a trustline and view issued tokens, teaching how digital assets are managed in a secure, permission-based way. To activate a new Xaman account, beginners must transfer a small amount of XRP from an exchange such as Coinbase. This process itself is educational, showing how value moves from a centralized exchange into self-custody and how wallets become active participants on a blockchain network.

Flare also integrates with MetaMask, giving beginners a chance to experience something different: delegation. By holding FLR tokens and connecting through MetaMask, users can delegate to Flare's decentralized data providers. This not only supports the network's ability to bring real-world data on-chain but also allows participants to earn rewards in return. It is a simple but powerful way to see how blockchain creates utility beyond speculation.

Together, these steps provide a clear, hands-on path into decentralized applications, from finance to creativity, from asset management to data participation, showing how blockchain use cases are already unfolding in practice.

Exploring identity solutions

Identity is one of the most powerful frontiers of blockchain. For centuries, identity was controlled by governments, banks, and corporations that decided who qualified and held the records. Blockchain is shifting this balance by giving individuals the ability to own their digital identity directly: portable, verifiable, and secure.

With **MetaMask**, beginners can try Sign-In with Ethereum, logging in to apps with their wallet instead of creating usernames and passwords. This small step shows how identity can be linked to a wallet they control rather than a company account.

Coinbase Wallet makes it even easier to explore verifiable credentials. Many events, communities, and online courses issue blockchain-based badges or proof-of-attendance tokens. Beginners connect their wallet, tap "Claim," and the credential appears automatically in the wallet's NFT tab. To keep the process free or very low-cost, most projects issue these credentials on the Polygon network, which Coinbase Wallet supports with just a simple network switch. This means beginners can gain their first credential without facing expensive Ethereum fees.

Polygon ID demonstrates the next step in privacy-preserving verification. With it, a person can prove they are over 18 without sharing their full birthdate, or show they belong to a specific community without giving up personal details. These small but powerful demonstrations highlight how blockchain transforms identity from something managed by others to something individuals own and control themselves.

These early steps demonstrate something profound: identity on blockchain moves from something issued and controlled by others to something held securely by the individual. Today it may be a proof-of-attendance badge, but the same process can soon apply to diplomas, certifications, or professional memberships, credentials that individuals own and share directly.

Mindset shifts are equally important. Decentralization requires greater personal responsibility. Custody of assets, understanding of protocols, and participation in communities often rest with the individual. The tradeoff for freedom and inclusion is accountability and learning.

Business Preparation: Adapting to Decentralized Ecosystems

For companies, decentralization changes competitive landscapes and customer expectations. Businesses must understand not only how blockchain disrupts supply chains, payments, and compliance but also how customers increasingly value transparency, direct engagement, and proof of authenticity.

Key areas of preparation include:

- **Finance and operations.** Multinationals like JPMorgan and Citi are piloting tokenized deposits and settlement platforms, showing that even the largest financial institutions are adapting. Businesses that ignore tokenized finance may face higher costs and slower operations compared to those that adopt.

- **Supply chain accountability.** IBM and Maersk pioneered blockchain for logistics, and companies like De Beers and Everledger are applying it to verify ethical sourcing. Firms in industries from fashion to food must prepare for a future where consumers expect blockchain-based proof of sustainability.

- **Customer engagement.** Brands like Nike and Starbucks are using blockchain to connect loyalty programs, digital collectibles, and real-world purchases. This shift is not about novelty but about building communities of engaged participants rather than passive customers.

- **Compliance and governance.** Businesses must prepare for evolving regulations on digital assets, identity, and data. Europe's MiCA framework and U.S.

state-level regulations highlight the need for proactive strategy rather than reactive compliance.

Preparing for decentralization as a business means moving beyond pilots into integration, aligning strategy, operations, and culture with distributed models.

Government Preparation: Regulating and Adopting

Governments face both the challenge and the opportunity of decentralization. The challenge lies in balancing innovation with risk, protecting consumers while fostering growth. The opportunity lies in using blockchain themselves to provide more transparent and efficient public services.

Several examples highlight this path:

- **Dubai** has built blockchain into dozens of government services, from property transactions to licensing.

- **Estonia** has secured healthcare, property, and judicial registries on blockchain, creating a digital governance model admired worldwide.

- **The United States** has piloted blockchain for pharmaceutical traceability and vehicle titles, while states like Wyoming and Texas are experimenting with digital asset frameworks.

- **The European Union** is integrating blockchain across member services through the European Blockchain Services Infrastructure.

Preparing for decentralization as a government means not only regulating markets but also leading by example in transparency, accountability, and efficiency.

Opportunities for Participation

Decentralization opens doors for participation that extend beyond financial markets. Individuals can contribute skills to decentralized autonomous organizations (DAOs), support open-source development, or engage in decentralized science (DeSci) initiatives. Artists and musicians can mint work on-chain and connect with global audiences directly. Citizens can use decentralized identity to control access to their records, from health data to educational diplomas.

Examples already underway include Gitcoin, which has distributed millions in funding for open-source projects; ConstitutionDAO, which mobilized thousands of people to collectively bid on a historic U.S. artifact; and platforms like Rally and Mirror that allow creators to monetize communities directly.

Participation does not require large investments. It requires willingness to explore, experiment, and engage. The decentralized world rewards initiative and collaboration.

Risks and Responsibilities

While opportunities are vast, preparation must also account for risks. Decentralization does not eliminate the need for trust; it redistributes it. Code can fail, protocols can be hacked, and communities can fracture. Without intermediaries, individuals and businesses carry greater responsibility for due diligence, custody, and decision-making.

Well-publicized incidents, such as exchange collapses or poorly governed DAOs, remind us that decentralization is not a guarantee of fairness or safety. Preparing responsibly means combining enthusiasm with caution. Verifying platforms, diversifying risks, and advocating for standards that protect participants without stifling innovation.

The Human Dimension

Preparing for a decentralized world ultimately comes back to people. It is about creating systems where inclusion, accountability, and opportunity are not controlled by the few but accessible to the many. It is about recognizing that the skills we choose to build, the systems we choose to support, and the communities we choose to engage with will shape how decentralization unfolds.

This preparation is not passive. It requires vision, adaptability, and participation. The decentralized world is being built now, and those who engage early will not only benefit but also influence its trajectory.

Key Takeaways

• Decentralization redistributes trust from central authorities to code, consensus, and cryptography.

• Individuals can prepare by learning digital literacy skills such as wallets, decentralized apps, and identity tools.

• Businesses must adapt operations, supply chains, and customer engagement to meet expectations of transparency and accountability.

• Governments face the dual task of regulating digital assets while adopting blockchain for their own services.

• Opportunities for participation range from DAOs and DeSci to creative industries and community-driven initiatives.

• Risks remain, requiring caution, due diligence, and responsible governance.

• Preparation is about more than technology—it is about mindset, inclusion, and active participation.

Reflection Questions

1. How prepared are you personally to manage digital assets, decentralized identity, or blockchain-based services?

2. What opportunities exist in your field to adopt decentralized models for efficiency or transparency?

3. How could your organization prepare today for the shift to tokenized finance, supply chains, or customer engagement?

4. Where could you participate in decentralized communities or initiatives that align with your skills and values?

5. What responsibilities come with participating in decentralized systems, and how will you approach them?

Chapter 33

The Beginning of Everything: A Final Note on Vision, Growth, and Empowerment

A closing reflection on why understanding this technology now means stepping boldly into the future with knowledge, purpose, and power.

Every era has a defining moment when humanity's systems evolve, and individuals are invited to rise with them. The shift into a decentralized world is one of those moments. What began as obscure lines of code has grown into a living network of trust, transparency, and participation that reaches into every aspect of life. Understanding blockchain today is not about following a trend, it is about aligning with the foundation of tomorrow.

At its core, blockchain is not only about money or markets. It is about redefining how we coordinate, how we prove truth, how we participate, and how we grow. From the way governments secure records, to how businesses issue contracts, to how individuals build wealth and identity, the adoption of blockchain signals a structural realignment of society. Those who understand it early are not simply informed, they are empowered to shape the systems that others will later adapt to.

Vision: Seeing What Comes Before It Arrives

Throughout history, progress has belonged to those who could see ahead. The printing press unlocked literacy before most could imagine its reach. The internet reshaped communication so quickly that some governments and businesses were left unprepared. Today, blockchain sits in that same position, emerging quietly as the rails of the future while many still debate its relevance.

Vision is the ability to recognize that what looks experimental now will soon be ordinary. Just as email replaced letters and online banking replaced paper ledgers, blockchain based systems are becoming invisible infrastructure. Payments will settle instantly. Credentials will be verified in seconds. Supply chains will be transparent from end to end. For those who can see it, the future has already begun.

Growth: Building Capacity Through Participation

The growth opportunity is not only financial. Growth here means expanding capacity, the ability to operate with clarity, trust, and reach. Blockchain allows an entrepreneur in Lagos to access the same financial tools as a developer in London. It gives a student in India the chance to own their educational credentials and carry them anywhere. It lets a farmer in South America prove where their crops were grown and receive fair compensation.

These are not isolated benefits. They are multipliers. Each person who gains access expands the network's value for everyone else. Growth becomes collective, not exclusive. The more we participate, the more resilient and connected the system becomes.

Empowerment: Moving from Users to Owners

The most profound shift blockchain offers is empowerment. In centralized systems, people are users, dependent on the terms, timelines, and permissions of intermediaries. In decentralized systems, people are owners of their data, their assets, and their choices. This is not an abstract promise, it is visible today.

Artists sell their work directly to global audiences without gatekeepers. Communities create their own economies and govern themselves transparently. Citizens in nations with unstable currencies preserve value through stablecoins. Investors access tokenized shares of real estate or funds without needing traditional brokers. Each example reflects the same underlying truth: blockchain redistributes power by aligning ownership with participation.

The Role of Companies and Institutions

Global companies and institutions are already signaling that blockchain is here to stay. BlackRock is piloting tokenized funds that operate on blockchain rails. The European Investment Bank issues bonds on Ethereum. IBM, Accenture, and Deloitte are building blockchain solutions for supply chain and enterprise trust. Governments from the United States to Singapore are embedding blockchain in public services.

When the world's most established organizations commit resources to a technology, it confirms the direction of travel. But unlike past technological shifts, this one is not reserved for institutions. The tools are open, the knowledge is available, and the entry points are accessible to anyone with a smartphone and an internet connection. The door to empowerment is wide, and it is open.

A Personal Decision: How You Step Into the Future

Understanding blockchain is not about predicting markets or memorizing technical jargon. It is about choosing how you want to participate in the systems that will define the next generation. Do you want to be informed, or dependent? Do you want to shape, or adapt?

For some, this journey will begin by learning to use a wallet. For others, it will mean exploring decentralized applications, claiming their first digital credential, or supporting sustainable supply chains through blockchain based verification. Each step is valuable because each step moves you closer to participation, ownership, and empowerment.

The shift is not about technology alone. It is about mindset. It is about embracing the responsibility that comes with holding your own assets, making your own decisions, and verifying truth directly. This responsibility may feel daunting at first, but it is also liberating. It transforms individuals from passive recipients of systems into active contributors to them.

The Beginning of Everything

The title of this chapter is deliberate. While the book is concluding, the journey it describes is only beginning. Blockchain is not the end of something old, it is the beginning of something entirely new. The beginning of systems that respect transparency. The beginning of communities that align ownership with participation. The beginning of individuals who step forward with clarity, purpose, and power.

Each generation faces a choice about whether to accept the world as it is or to participate in creating the world that comes next. With blockchain, the choice is clear. The future will not be built only by governments or corporations, it will be built by every individual who chooses to learn, to engage, and to step forward.

This is not the closing of a book. It is the opening of a door. What comes next is yours to shape.

Key Takeaways

• Blockchain represents a structural realignment of society, shifting power from centralized authorities to individuals and communities

• Vision is recognizing that blockchain's emerging systems will soon be everyday infrastructure

• Growth comes through collective participation, where each new user expands the network's value

• Empowerment is moving from being a user of systems to being an owner of assets, data, and choices

• Global companies and governments confirm blockchain's permanence, but its tools remain open to everyone

• This is not the end of something old, it is the beginning of everything new

---

Reflection Questions

1. How do you personally define empowerment, and how might blockchain expand that definition for you?

2. What first step could you take to participate more actively in decentralized systems?

3. Where do you see the greatest opportunity for collective growth through blockchain participation?

4. How can you balance the responsibility of ownership with the opportunities it creates?

5. What role do you want to play in shaping the systems that will define the next generation?

Glossary

Acciona – A global infrastructure company that uses blockchain to certify renewable energy usage in its projects. (Chapter 27)

Address – A unique string of letters and numbers that identifies a wallet on a blockchain, used to send and receive digital assets. (Chapter 2)

Altcoin – Any cryptocurrency other than Bitcoin. (Chapter 2)

Alternative Asset – Any non-traditional investment outside stocks and bonds, such as real estate, art, or tokenized collectibles. (Chapter 8)

Alternative Trading System (ATS) – A regulated marketplace that allows compliant secondary trading of digital securities outside of traditional stock exchanges. (Chapter 26)

AMM (Automated Market Maker) – A decentralized exchange mechanism that uses liquidity pools and algorithms instead of order books to enable trading. (Chapter 8)

Asset Token – A digital representation of a real-world asset, such as real estate, commodities, or goods in a supply chain. Unlike cryptocurrencies, asset tokens are tied to the value or details of something physical or financial. (Chapter 4)

Atomic Settlement – The instantaneous exchange of assets where both sides of a transaction settle simultaneously, removing counterparty risk. (Chapter 26)

Bitcoin – The first and most widely used cryptocurrency, created in 2009 by the pseudonymous Satoshi Nakamoto. It operates on a decentralized network secured by Proof of Work and is often described as digital gold. (Chapter 2)

Block – A data unit in the blockchain that contains a list of transactions, a timestamp, and a reference (hash) to the previous block. (Chapter 1)

Blockchain – A decentralized digital ledger that records transactions in blocks linked together chronologically, creating a transparent and immutable history. (Chapter 1)

Blockchain Economy – The system of value creation, exchange, and services powered by blockchain technology, where tokens represent money, assets, identity, or access, and flow through networks to enable transactions and automation. (Chapter 4)

Bond Tokenization – The process of issuing traditional bonds, such as government or corporate debt, on blockchain for faster settlement and broader participation. (Chapter 27)

Carbon Credit – A tradable permit representing one ton of carbon dioxide removed or avoided, increasingly tokenized, and tracked on blockchain systems. (Chapter 26)

CBDC (Central Bank Digital Currency) – A digital version of a nation's currency issued and regulated by its central bank. (Chapter 12)

Central Bank – A nation's primary financial authority, such as the Federal Reserve, that issues currency and regulates monetary policy. (Chapter 12)

CFC Rewards DApp – A decentralized application within the Center for Creators ecosystem that allows participants to earn and redeem CFC Tokens through activities tied to personal growth, education, work, or community engagement. (Chapter 17)

CFC Token – A blockchain-based utility token created on the XRP Ledger to power the Center for Creators ecosystem. It enables participants to claim and redeem value across publishing, education, workplace, lifestyle, and community-based applications. (Chapter 17)

Coinbase – A United States based exchange and wallet provider. Coinbase Wallet is referenced in the book for hands-on experiences like NFTs and digital credentials. (Chapter 8)

Cold Wallet – A cryptocurrency wallet kept offline (such as hardware wallets like Ledger or Trezor) for maximum security. (Chapter 32)

Collateral – Assets pledged as security for a loan or credit line, which can be liquidated if repayment obligations are not met. (Chapter 7)

Conscious AI – Artificial intelligence designed and integrated with ethical frameworks to personalize growth, learning, and collaboration in ways aligned with human well-being and values. (Chapter 17)

Consensus Mechanism – The method blockchain networks use to agree on the state of the ledger, such as Proof of Work or Proof of Stake. (Chapter 3)

Cryptocurrency – A digital currency that uses cryptography for security and operates on decentralized networks like blockchain. (Chapter 2)

Currency Token – A blockchain-based digital representation of money, often in the form of stablecoins, used for payments and settlements. (Chapter 4)

Custodian – A regulated entity that securely holds digital assets on behalf of institutions or individuals. (Chapter 26)

DAO (Decentralized Autonomous Organization) – An organization governed by rules encoded on blockchain, where decisions are made by token holders through transparent voting. (Chapter 14)

De Beers – A global diamond company that uses blockchain through its Tracr platform to verify ethical sourcing of diamonds. (Chapter 25)

DeFi (Decentralized Finance) – A system of financial applications built on blockchain that operate without intermediaries like banks. (Chapter 7)

Delegation (Flare) – Assigning FLR tokens to Flare's decentralized data providers to support the network while earning rewards. (Chapter 32)

Digital Certificate of Authenticity – A blockchain record verifying the authenticity and provenance of goods such as luxury items or art. (Chapter 25)

Digital Identity – A verifiable identity managed by an individual using blockchain-based credentials. (Chapter 32)

Digital Securities – Tokenized forms of traditional assets such as stocks or bonds issued and traded on blockchain. (Chapter 26)

Digital Twin – A digital asset created on a blockchain to represent a real-world product or item, such as a shipment of lettuce, including all its details and history. (Chapter 4)

Emission Tracking – Recording greenhouse gas data across supply chains, often tied to blockchain-based sustainability verification. (Chapter 27)

Ethereum – A leading blockchain platform that enables smart contracts and decentralized applications. (Chapter 4)

European Investment Bank (EIB) – The EU's lending arm and an early issuer of blockchain-based bonds, signaling mainstream institutional adoption. (Chapter 27)

Everledger – A technology company that uses blockchain to track provenance and authenticity of valuable assets like diamonds and luxury goods. (Chapter 25)

Fiat Currency – Government-issued money, such as the U.S. dollar or euro. (Chapter 2)

Flare – A blockchain network that integrates with MetaMask, enabling delegation of tokens and providing real-time data feeds to applications. (Chapter 32)

Food and Drug Administration (FDA) – A U.S. agency that piloted blockchain to improve pharmaceutical supply chain traceability. (Chapter 31)

Gas Fees – Transaction fees paid to process and validate operations on blockchain networks like Ethereum. (Chapter 4)

Halving – An event in Bitcoin where mining rewards are reduced by half, slowing new issuance and affecting supply dynamics. (Chapter 4)

Hash – A unique cryptographic fingerprint generated for each block, ensuring the integrity and order of transactions. (Chapter 1)

Holcim – One of the world's largest cement producers, piloting blockchain to track emissions and recycled material use. (Chapter 27)

IBM (IBM Food Trust) – A global technology company. Its blockchain platform, IBM Food Trust, is used for traceability in supply chains and later adapted for construction. (Chapter 27)

Immersive Environment (Metaverse) – A virtual, blockchain-integrated space where participants can interact, learn, and create together, often using tokens or NFTs for access and ownership. (Chapter 17)

Immutable – A characteristic of blockchain meaning records cannot be altered once confirmed. (Chapter 1)

Identity Verification (KYC) – The "Know Your Customer" process mentioned in compliance contexts, where users prove their identity before accessing services. (Chapter 26)

Initial Coin Offering (ICO) – A method of raising capital by selling tokens in exchange for funding. (Chapter 6)

Internet of Things (IoT) – Networks of connected devices, often integrated with blockchain for real-time verification. (Chapter 27)

JPMorgan Chase (Onyx and JPM Coin) – A major bank referenced for blockchain settlement pilots and tokenized payments through its Onyx platform and JPM Coin. (Chapter 8)

Ledger – A record of transactions. In blockchain, it is distributed across many participants. (Chapter 1)

Liquidity Pool – Funds locked into a smart contract that enable decentralized trading and yield opportunities. (Chapter 8)

Maersk (TradeLens) – A global shipping company cited for TradeLens, which digitized and secured shipping documentation with blockchain. (Chapter 28)

MetaMask – A widely used digital wallet that allows users to connect to decentralized applications. (Chapter 32)

Micropayment – A very small digital transaction, often made practical by blockchain due to low fees. (Chapter 12)

Miner – A participant in Proof of Work blockchains who uses computing power to solve puzzles and validate blocks, earning rewards in tokens. (Chapter 3)

NFT (Non-Fungible Token) – A unique digital token representing ownership of a specific asset such as art, collectibles, or real estate. (Chapter 5)

Node – A computer that participates in the blockchain network by storing a copy of the ledger and verifying transactions. (Chapter 1)

On-Chain Publishing – The use of blockchain to mint books, articles, or creative works as NFTs, providing verifiable ownership, authenticity, and potential access to exclusive content. (Chapter 17)

Oracle – A service that brings real-world data into blockchain applications for use in smart contracts. (Chapter 9)

Permissioned Blockchain – A blockchain where participation is restricted to approved users, often used by enterprises. (Chapter 27)

Polygon ID – A privacy-preserving identity solution that enables verification without oversharing personal data. (Chapter 32)

Private Key – A secret cryptographic code that allows the owner to access and manage digital assets. (Chapter 2)

Programmable Asset – Similar to programmable money but referring to tokenized assets with built-in rules for how they can be transferred or used. (Chapter 10)

Programmable Money – Digital currency with logic for automated distribution or restrictions. (Chapter 10)

Provenance – The verified history of an asset's origin and ownership, often tracked on blockchain for supply chains, art, and luxury goods. (Chapter 25)

Public Blockchain – An open blockchain network that anyone can access. (Chapter 2)

Remittances – Cross-border money transfers, often sent by migrant workers, made faster and cheaper with blockchain. (Chapter 12)

Repo (Repurchase Agreement) – A short-term borrowing arrangement in traditional finance, referenced when discussing tokenized treasuries. (Chapter 26)

Ripple – A fintech company that developed the XRP Ledger, referenced for payments, remittances, and institutional settlement. (Chapter 8)

Satoshi Nakamoto – The pseudonymous creator of Bitcoin who published its whitepaper in 2008. (Chapter 1)

Secondary Market – A marketplace where digital securities or tokenized assets can be traded after their initial issuance. (Chapter 26)

Secondary Trading – The resale of tokenized assets after their initial issuance, a point made in the capital markets discussion. (Chapter 26)

Skanska – A European construction company experimenting with blockchain for contract management and materials verification. (Chapter 27)

Smart Contract – Self-executing code on blockchain that automatically enforces conditions once met. (Chapter 3)

Smart Contract Automation – Programs on the blockchain that automatically trigger actions (such as releasing payments or updating records) when conditions are met. (Chapter 4)

Stablecoin – A cryptocurrency pegged to a stable asset such as the U.S. dollar. (Chapter 12)

Stellar (Stellar Development Foundation) – A nonprofit supporting the Stellar blockchain, known for cross-border payments and financial inclusion use cases. (Chapter 8)

Streaming Payments – Real-time distribution of wages or revenue using blockchain. (Chapter 26)

Synthetic Asset – A blockchain-based token designed to

mimic the value of another asset (like a stock, commodity, or currency). (Chapter 26)

Timestamp – A record of the exact time a transaction is added to a block, ensuring transparency and chronological order. (Chapter 1)

Token – A digital unit of value created on a blockchain that can represent rights, assets, or access. (Chapter 2)

Token-Gated Access – A blockchain-based method of granting entry to programs, events, or services by requiring participants to hold a specific token. This ensures authenticity, loyalty, and verified participation. (Chapter 17)

Tokenization – The process of creating blockchain-based digital representations of real-world assets. (Chapter 8)

Transaction – The basic action recorded on a blockchain, representing the transfer of value, data, or rights between parties. (Chapter 1)

Transparency – A feature of blockchain where all transactions are visible and verifiable. (Chapter 1)

Treasury (DAO or Corporate) – A pool of funds managed collectively, often tokenized, and governed on-chain in decentralized organizations. (Chapter 14 & 26)

Trustline – On the XRP Ledger, a feature that lets wallets approve which token issuers they trust. (Chapter 19)

Turner Construction – A U.S. construction firm exploring blockchain to streamline project contracts. (Chapter 27)

Uniswap – A decentralized exchange on Ethereum that enables peer-to-peer token swaps. (Chapter 32)

Utility Token – A token that provides access to a product or service in a blockchain ecosystem. (Chapter 6)

Validator – A participant in a Proof of Stake blockchain who verifies transactions and adds them to the ledger. (Chapter 3)

Verifiable Credential – A blockchain-based certificate proving identity, qualifications, or participation. (Chapter 32)

Visa – A global payments company highlighted for stablecoin settlement pilots and blockchain integrations. (Chapter 8)

Walmart – A multinational retailer that uses blockchain to trace provenance and safety in supply chains. (Chapter 28)

Wallet – A digital tool for storing and managing cryptocurrencies and tokens. (Chapter 2)

Web3 – A vision of a decentralized internet where users own their data, assets, and identity. (Chapter 4)

Whitelisting – A process of pre-approving wallets for blockchain-based offerings. (Chapter 26)

World Bank – A multilateral institution that has issued blockchain-based bonds, signaling public sector trust in the technology. (Chapter 27)

Xaman Wallet – A wallet for the XRP Ledger enabling trustlines, token management, and decentralized application access. (Chapter 32)

XRP Ledger (XRPL) – A decentralized blockchain designed for fast, low-cost transactions and token issuance. (Chapter 2)

Yield – The earnings generated from blockchain activities like lending, staking, or liquidity provision. (Chapter 26)

Zero-Knowledge Proof (ZKP) – A cryptographic method that allows one party to prove knowledge of information without revealing it. (Chapter 32)

About the Author

Christie Russ is the only authority who helps leaders align with their highest purpose by merging with blockchain, AI, crypto, and next-gen technology. Creating industry-shifting legacies and future-defining systems built on clarity, alignment, and intelligent expansion.

She is the #1 Amazon bestselling author of *The Power to Rise*, a book that climbed to the top of Amazon charts in less than a month of publication. She turns transformation into direct decentralized value, linking readers to her CFC Rewards DApp where they claim CFC Tokens for taking aligned action.

Christie launched the CFC Token in 2021, and within its first two weeks it went viral, landing in the top 1% out of over 9,300 tokens on the XRPL. It was a demonstration of how communities can build new economies by converging personal evolution with blockchain innovation.

She later created the Pickleball Coin, a decentralized tool that enables clubs to fund new facilities and strengthen operations without giving up ownership stakes, while rewarding supporters and players through community-driven token systems.

As founder of the Center for Creators (CFC), Christie architects ecosystems that empower creators, entrepreneurs, and innovators to monetize loyalty, build community-driven value, and scale beyond traditional gatekeepers. She integrates blockchain, crypto, AI, and next-generation systems to help them design conscious, future-focused frameworks that elevate both their ventures and the communities they serve.

Her platform Blockchain for Beginners, along with her upcoming book *Blockchain Made Simple*, positions Christie as the trusted authority for leaders who want to leverage blockchain, crypto, AI and advanced technologies as strategic tools for building purpose-driven legacies.

What sets Christie entirely apart is that she is the only authority who teaches blockchain, AI and crypto through the lens of personal energetic mastery, integrating it all with her frameworks for decentralized creator economies, rewards systems, and leading-edge technologies like metaverse environments, avatars, and holograms. It's why top founders, investors, and other blockchain projects turn to her when they need the clearest strategy grounded in both energetic alignment and scalable tech.

Her personal story mirrors the radical expansion she builds for others. Having never played sports before, Christie took up pickleball at 56 and, within two years, reached the 4.0 competitive level. Utilizing AI, and hard work to accelerate her game. Qualifying for the semi-annual 2025 National Senior Olympics. It's a testament to how quickly mastery manifests when her principles of alignment and execution are in motion.

Through private advisory and bespoke Legacy Blueprints, Christie guides high-level leaders to align with their highest purpose and create ventures rooted in abundance, balance, and meaningful, purpose-driven impact.

She is sought out by global innovators, founders, and visionary communities who recognize her rare ability to merge personal evolution with decentralized technology — empowering them to shape lives, businesses, and legacies that transform industries and redefine the future.

Everything Christie does serves one unwavering mission:

To architect futures where human evolution and next-generation systems converge, elevating lives, communities, and the legacies that will shape tomorrow.

ChristieRuss.com

CenterForCreators.com

CFCRewards.com

LinkedIn: @christie-jackmond-russ

Note to the Reader

This book exists because of you. The encouragement, questions, and inspiration that came through my *Blockchain for Beginners* series shaped every page that followed. Your curiosity and willingness to learn pushed me to expand these conversations into something bigger, something that could serve as both a guide and a companion for anyone stepping into this new digital era.

My hope is that as you move through these chapters, you feel not only informed but also empowered, ready to see yourself as part of this transformation rather than standing on the sidelines. I wrote this book to explain blockchain in ways everyone can understand, so no one feels excluded from the opportunities ahead. The future of blockchain is not distant or abstract. It is already here, and your participation matters.

With gratitude and purpose,
Christie Russ

Join Center for Creators Community on the CFC Rewards App

Claim and Redeem CFC Tokens for taking actionable steps!

www.ingramcontent.com/pod-product-compliance
Lightning Source LLC
Chambersburg PA
CBHW071316210326
41597CB00015B/1244